The Art of Being Deaf

Being Deaf

1-56368-598-9

en--Australia--

ITY PRESS

Gallaudet University Press
Washington, DC 20002
http://gupress.gallaudet.edu

Library of Congress Cataloging-in-Publication Data

McDonald, Donna, 1955-
   The art of being deaf : a memoir / Donna McDonald.
      pages cm
   Includes bibliographical references.
    ISBN 978-1-56368-597-2 (pbk. : alk. paper) -- ISBN (invalid) 978
(e-book)
 1. McDonald, Donna, 1955- 2. Deaf--Australia--Biography. 3. Deaf wom
Biography. I. Title.
   HV2943.M33A3 2014
   362.4'2092--dc23
   [B]

                         2013042489

Cover art and design by Donna Wright.

Some of the names in this memoir have been changed.

The whole body was removed
From the vibration of air, they lived through the eyes
The clear simple look, the instant full attention.
—Ted Hughes, "Deaf School"

Long-continued disability makes some people saintly, some
self-pitying, some bitter. It has only clarified Sally and made
her more herself.
—Wallace Stegner, *Crossing to Safety*

Love is a central theme in the autobiography we each write as we try
to understand our lives; but we may feel that we become only more
confused the more we reflect upon it.
—John Armstrong, *Conditions of Love: The Philosophy of Intimacy*

Gratitude is the memory of the heart.
—Jean Massieu, 1772–1846, deaf student and teacher in France

Contents

PART THREE

Prologue

Through the Eyes of a Child

If you had been walking across the William Jolley Bridge that sultry February morning, and if you had been looking out for it, you would have seen a cream-colored car with absinthe-green panels. A new 1957 Holden, it pointed south toward the Oral Deaf Preschool at Yeronga, a suburb of Brisbane, in Queensland, Australia. You would not have understood the significance of its journey at the time. Not even the participants in that journey could have reasonably anticipated what would follow in the years to come. The car was heading not just to a school, but to an entire new world of opportunity, a world that promised spoken speech as well as an education for little deaf children.

The driver of the car was my mother, a thirty-three-year-old woman with dark brown hair. She wore black-rimmed, bat-wing-style glasses that framed her olive-green eyes. The fierceness of her glasses was softened by her summer frock with its pattern of roses and a cinched waist. My mother looked ahead of the car in front of her and saw that the pace of the traffic had faltered. She pulled on the car's gearstick and tapped her fingers impatiently on the steering wheel.

I sat in the back seat of that car. I was three years old and had wispy blonde hair and a dimple in my left cheek when I smiled. But now my chin was crumpled in a fury of crying. A breeze filtered through the open windows. It lifted my hair off my forehead but did not ease the red flush of my face. My cries must have sounded like the tearing of metal. My shrieks ebbed into the defeat of hiccoughs before gathering new strength for another onslaught of rage. I grabbed my left ear as if to peel it from my head. A pink button was pushed into its ridges and hollows. The plastic cord dangling from it was attached to a metal box the size of a cigarette pack, encased in the pocket of a grey gabardine shoulder harness strapped around my body. I yanked at the cord once, my hand whitening with the effort. I yanked it again, and then I gave it the hardest yank of all.

My mother heard the catch of breath and glanced up at the rearview mirror just in time to see the pink button wrenched free from my ear. It popped out with a force that launched it up, up, and out, out into the air beyond the car window. The button's cord traced a glorious arc before falling beneath the wheels of the cars behind us. I rested my head against the sticky vinyl of the car seat, my hair still fluttering in the breeze, my sea-green eyes blinking against the white clouds of softness falling into my ears.

PART ONE

1

Deaf

When I choose to turn my hearing aids off and so switch off the world of sounds, I experience delicious relief. It is as if a sigh is breathing into my ears. My shoulders relax from their "pinned to the ears" position of strain. My face relaxes. Everything in me relaxes. I don't feel on alert to the world; I do not feel on guard. I am at home in my silence, free to fill it up with my own sounds—the sounds of memories, reveries, and hopes.

But I feel this only if the closure of sound is of my choosing: I panic if I am out and about and my hearing aids fail me in some way. I feel unsafe then, as if I have been blinded by a mudslide that I cannot find my way through. When I turn my hearing aids back on, the air momentarily becomes harsh and stinging. In that split second when sound crashes against silence, I must reengage with my world. I have to adapt each time, but once having adapted, I enjoy the return of the loud and the soft, the bellow and the whisper, the variety of sounds in all their musicality and clamor.

I was already feeling the strain of the appointment when the psychologist asked his question, in the form of a statement: "Your hearing loss must have had a big impact on you?"

I hesitated.

He turned it into a refrain. "Your deafness? It must have been difficult?" Dust motes hung in the arrow of sunshine between us. He sat in a shadowy corner of the timber-paneled room, and I slouched in a low-slung chair beneath a cracked window. The distance between us was as vast as the Nullabor Plain, as arid as the Simpson Desert. The force of the psychologist's words was muffled by his beard, fluffed up around his mouth and blurring the outlines of his words. Lipreading him from so far across the room was like trying to read fading print. I could make out the vowel sounds, but was that a "p" or a "b"? I stretched and flexed my fingers to release the tension in them, and closed my eyes for a few seconds. I struggled to sit up straight. The psychologist ran his right index finger around the inside of his shirt collar as if it was strangling him. His question hung in the air along with the dust motes. I used my arms to pull myself upright in the chair again and cast around for a way to deflect the psychologist's question.

I was forty-five years old, but a childish refusal welled up in my chest. I did not want to answer this question. The bluntness of it offended me. It had lunged at me without warning, winding me. I had already answered many questions as precisely as I could about my work, for this was the reason I was there in his office. A social worker friend, Jennifer, had urged me to see him. We had worked together in disability policy on and off for fifteen years, and she had observed my mounting distress about the gap between my achievements in my public service career and my disappointments in romantic relationships.

I said to the psychologist, "Not really."

Short silence. I tried again. "Perhaps?"

No response. Clearing of my throat. Stalling for more time. "What was the question again?"

"Your deafness. It must surely have had a profound impact on you as you were growing up."

No rising inflection this time. A declamatory statement infused with a sort of restrained anger. I imagined the thought bubble floating above his head, "Must I repeat everything?" But I had no sympathy for him.

His question didn't just offend me. It irritated me, felt voyeuristic. I could not see its relevance to my work stress. It was a variation on a theme; I had been asked versions of this question all my life, usually followed by the crude and presumptuous statement that "being deaf must be terrible for you." Because I fell into that shadow-land category of "oral-deaf"—I could not hear without my hearing aids, but I did not communicate by signing with my hands; I could speak with my voice—I would also be asked, "What sort of deaf person are you?" After all these years and all these questions, I still found it difficult to summon up an off-the-cuff answer that would satisfy both me and the person doing the asking. If I went against my grain and said, "Yes, being deaf has had a big impact on my life," the questioner would quiz me with inquisitorial precision, heedless of my feelings about being the object of such scrutiny. If I said no, injecting a note of warning into my voice not to pursue the topic, the questioner would acquire an expression of hauteur and assume he (it was usually a "he") had the obligation to help me to "face facts" by reciting a list of "what if" scenarios.

I accepted that my life was different in some ways because of my deafness, but the differences did not seem to be particularly plentiful or exceptional. When I was three years old, I went to a school for deaf children, which I attended until I was eight years old; I was then transferred to a "normal" school. As I grew up, I had to make adjustments from time to time. I sat toward the front of classrooms at school and, later, at work conferences to make sure I could see to hear; and I disliked dimmed lighting, whether it was at a fireside campsite, in a restaurant, or on a friend's back deck because it put my companions' faces in shadow. I thought that was about it really. I was tongue-tied and reluctant to share any of this with the psychologist.

I decided to agree with him. "Oh yes, a big impact." I could not think of anything else to say that he might like to hear and that I was prepared to reveal, but it was the right tack to take, because he dropped the subject. We spent the last ten minutes of the appointment tossing around ideas for managing my work stress. He told me that I needed to meditate every now and then throughout the day, and that it would be good if I could go for a walk each morning to clear my head. I smiled at him.

I walked down the hill from Wickham Terrace, through the city, back to my office on Mary Street, shaken by the certainty in the psychologist's voice. I was not obtuse. Of course I understood that I was different from others simply by dint of being deaf, but it was not something that I gave much thought to. I had other things on my mind. The psychologist had asked me an earlier question. "Have you had any trauma in your life?"

"Trauma?"

"Yes," his voice filled with insinuation. "Any significant harm?"

"No."

I did not tell him about my son, Jack. I did not have a track along which to lay down my words safely. Instead, I bent my head and saw that the flesh across my knuckles had started to loosen with age. I thought of the creamy touch of Jack's baby hands.

I could have recited the facts. Jack was twenty-two and a half weeks old when he died suddenly thirteen years earlier. He had been my solemn-faced baby boy; my chest ached each rare time he smiled at me. At the back of his head, a tuft of hair stuck up which I slicked with a lick to make it stick up even more. He liked to lean forward so that he could see his world open up before him; he would never sit back. I was thirty-two years old at the time, but still unprepared for the flurry and spin of my days and nights as my life expanded with the fullness of this baby of mine. And then grief came through my door, became my twin; my son hummed his last breath into the cold sky above his cot, and ghosted into my shadow child. I was unprepared, then, for the stillness, the silence without echoes, and the air-lessness that seeped into my bones, into my heart.

But these facts would not have told the whole story. I could not have explained to the psychologist how my sorrow felt like a heavy weight, but that I was reluctant to relieve myself of this pain. To do so seemed like an act of disloyalty to my son, and I preferred, instead, to adjust to its bulk somehow. I lived my life cautiously, as if that might make a difference. I worked hard, kept up my friendships, and was moderate in my diet, drink, and fitness schedules. Jack's father was long gone. After we buried our son at the Pinaroo Lawn Cemetery, we were unable to console each other. Instead, I fought him, not in blame but in an unceasing and desperate urge to kick my pain away, to give it another reason. Our struggle was terrible. He left me, unwilling to bear the gap in my arms, the tearing away of the flesh and blood that formed our son. I loved him and hoped his flight was temporary, but his absence stretched into years. He made a new life for himself, remarried, and had a new child. A daughter this time. My love for him drained away until there was nothing left at all.

I was afraid this made me a shallow woman, and I fretted about my apparent inability to keep love alive. Other men passed in and out of my life, but I could not muster the wherewithal to keep them close to me. I didn't like this. Despite my desire to be in a lifelong relationship, fear was my steady companion. This was no great surprise. Once bitten, twice shy; and I'd already been bitten more than once, having also survived the collapse of a brief marriage to a man of considerable charm but equivocal love long ago. My friends chivvied me along and tried to encourage me to enjoy all that was good in my life. When I revealed to one of them that I believed being in a relationship would provide me with a sense of history, an enduring constancy, he chided me, saying, "That has to come from within you. No one else can give you that."

I didn't go back to that psychologist. Instead, I dealt with my stress by getting involved in a new work project while knowing that I wanted to do something more dramatic. Something fresh. Perhaps freeing. Fabulous, even. I was single, lonely, and tired from the joyless diligence of my days. My torpor was crushing me, and so when someone I knew in England suggested that I apply for a job over there, I sent off my application as if it was a telegram of hope.

The odd thing was, I could not forget the certainty in the psychologist's voice. It haunted me. He had repeated his question about my deafness once more, rephrasing it for emphasis: "It must surely have had a profound impact on you as you were growing up." I felt unsettled by his words. I was assailed by doubt and wondered why I felt so jarred by a question that I had, for most of my life, shrugged off.

I mulled over the basic facts of my biography. I was the sole deaf child in a family of five muddling along during the 1950s and 1960s in a weatherboard war commission house at The Grange, a Brisbane suburb. It had closely mowed lawns, a creek at the bottom of a hill, a lolly shop crammed with God-knows-what other crazy trinkets, a bakery with faded awnings that sold white sponge cakes with pink icing, and a butcher shop with sawdust on the floor and slabs of beef with purple stamps on the skin strung up on long, grey steel hooks. The local milk-bar gave off a hopeful air of danger: young men in tight jeans—hair slicked back into a quiff with Brylcreem, and Craven A cigarette packs tucked up their T-shirt sleeves—hung out there; their ponytailed girlfriends were draped around them.

My father, Jimmy Mac, once a "Ledger Keeper" for the Mobil Vacuum Oil Company, had served as a corporal in the Australian Imperial Force (AIF) during World War II in Ceylon and New Guinea. He had also served as a boxing official at the 1956 Melbourne Olympic Games, having earlier won fame and been written up in the Brisbane *Courier Mail* as a "bright little bantamweight" and "one of the best lightweight boxers in North Queensland" with a "dandy left, and a good right [who] steps into his punches pivoting on them well." My memories of him stemmed from his days as a tally clerk on the wharves during the week and a bookie on Saturdays. Everywhere he went, he wore his felt hat with the little feather in the band. He would have worn it to shield his Irish complexion from the burn of the Queensland sun, but he probably also fancied it for its flair. He had a gift for telling stories that made people laugh. He even made himself laugh.

My mother, baptized Eloise but known to all as Jackie, was a curvily petite woman with a broad smile and green eyes that hinted at secrets she might share—if pressed—in exchange for a chat and a cigarette. She spent her childhood on a cherry orchard in Young before leaving at the age of fifteen to work as a nurse in wartime Sydney. Black-and-white prints snapped by roving photographers in the city streets at that time show her in the company of friends, all laughing as if life's comedy was theirs to enjoy forever. She met my father in North Queensland in one of those postwar romances when time was still an enemy of promise, and love had to be grasped in a quick foxtrot around the floor to the sound of a saxophone, lest it be swallowed up by yet another war, another Depression, another something terrible. Jimmy Mac sent Jackie a gilt-edged postcard—pink-golden sun setting on a palm-tree fringed beach—embossed with the words "Memories of Magnetic Island." On the back, he had written in his convent-bred penmanship, "Mine are happy. Are yours?"

After their wedding, they set up their home in Townsville and then moved to Brisbane two years later. My older sister, Cecily, wore her dark hair in thick Annie Oakley–style plaits and burnished her fair-skinned complexion with Coppertone lotion. My older brother, Michael, all sun-bleached hair and sturdy brown limbs, went on hikes along the Kedron Brook on summer days. My parents did not know of any deaf relatives in their families. There was just me, the little deaf girl, but I was not a child given to the moody contemplation of my deaf life. The fact that I wore a hearing aid and that my sister and brother did not was not remarkable to me. That was just the way things were.

Coincidentally, during this time of introspection, I was invited by an editor to write a piece for a literary journal, and so, with the psychologist's question still on my mind, I made it the trigger for an article. Still feeling defensive about his question, I wrote mockingly about the psychologist and presented my deaf childhood and adult life as a series of happy vignettes with only the occasional disruption to my sanguine self. I conceded, in this article, that I had missed my deaf childhood friends when I left them behind, that I had once experienced discrimination at university, and I wondered about the impact of my deafness on my sister and brother, as well as on my parents, but dealt with this in an "All's well that ends well" tone of dismissal. I wrote it more as a writing exercise than as an exhumation of the psychologist's question. The editor would not publish my article. He felt that I had gilded the lily, downplayed the significance of certain events, and avoided other questions altogether. He encouraged me to explore the topic more intently. While I wondered why this editor was so reluctant to accept my cheery version of events—must misery lurk in every story?—I accepted his challenge.

This was more difficult than I had expected. I do not go about the daily business of my life measuring how much I hear or do not hear, feeling barbs of revelation about my deaf self, and I wondered why it should be of such interest to anyone else. My being deaf is not usually the subject of self-absorption. I do not need to hear in order to think, and my private musings wander along the same topics as anyone else: work, relationships with friends and family, hopes and dreams about love. I can tune into my thoughts as soundless as they are. I like the muffled air of silence, and, in fact, I am writing all this with my hearing aids turned off; I enjoy the sense of being set apart from real life. But when I made myself consider the audiological facts of my deafness for this chapter, I was surprised by what I discovered.

I already knew that my deafness was unrelated to the rubella epidemic that had occurred during my mother's pregnancy, but I now learned that the opaque medical words used to define the absence or subduing of sound within me—"moderate-severe, sloping to profound, unknown etiology"—do not reveal what I can hear or cannot hear. For several days I experimented with sounds by tapping, clapping, and dropping things; by standing still on a busy footpath listening out for bird calls, people chatter, and car horns; and by turning my hearing aids on and off in different situations. I made notes about what I could or could not hear. I worked out that without my hearing aids, if I am concentrating, and if the sounds are made loudly, I am aware of those sounds at the lower end of the scale.

Sometimes, it is not so much that I can actually hear sounds; it's more that I know that those sounds are happening. My aural memory of the deep-register sounds helps me to "hear" them, much like the recollection of a tune replaying itself in my imagination. I discovered this effect during one of my sound experiments. I swim with friends regularly and had assumed that I could faintly hear the vowel sounds of their voices without my hearing aids. But one day, while I was talking with one of my swimming companions, I realized that I could not hear him at all. Nothing. Zilch. I had tricked even myself because I am so proficient at lipreading, and because I know what his voice sounds like when I wear my hearing aids. What I was actually doing was "dubbing" my friend's apparently soundless words with my recollection of his voice from our conversations when I wear my hearing aids.

With or without my hearing aids, if I am not watching the source of those sounds—for example, if the sounds are taking place in another room or even just behind me—I am not immediately able to distinguish whether the sounds are conversational or musical or happy or angry. I can only discriminate them once I have established the rhythm of the sounds; if the rhythm is at a tearing, jagged pace with an exaggerated rise and fall in the volume, I might reasonably assume that angry words are being had. I cannot hear high-pitched sounds at all, with or without my hearing aids: I cannot hear sibilants, the "cees" and "esses" and "zees." I cannot hear those sounds that bounce or puff off from your lips, such as the letters "b" and "p"; I cannot hear that sound that trampolines from the press of your tongue against the back of your front teeth, the letter "t." With hearing aids, I *can* hear and discriminate among the braying, hee-hawing, lilting, oohing, and twanging sounds of the vowels . . . but only if I am concentrating, and only if I am watching the source of the sounds. Without my hearing aids, I might also hear sharp and sudden sounds like the clap of hands or crash of plates, depending on the volume of the noise. But I cannot hear the ring of the telephone, or the chime of the doorbell, or the urgent siren of an ambulance speeding down the street.

My hearing aids help me to hear these sounds, but again, not all the time. I drift away from the pull of sound, and need others to tug me back. Many examples spring to mind, but one, from many years ago, will do for now. I have a nephew, Alexander who, as a six-year-old, was a serious-minded boy and not easily moved to laughter. He would reflect on the mysteries of arithmetic, posing such wonders as "Did you know that when you add up two odd numbers, the answers are always even?" One day, when I was driving him home from a children's theater, I glanced across at him in the passenger seat and saw he was grinning. He looked up at me, flushed with his smiles. I turned my attention back to the road, pleased by his enjoyment. A heartbeat later, Alexander called out in that over loud, barrel-chested voice of little boys. "Do you know that a police car is chasing us?" And that was how I caught the siren's heart-stopping, needy, wait-for-me cry.

I was curious about what it would mean for me if I reopened the psychologist's question for my private exploration. What *was* the impact of my deafness on my life? What threat would be posed to me if I tackled this question head-on? In the months following my visit to the psychologist, my reflections took on a more urgent, even querulous, tone. Having let the first questions to take hold in my imagination, new ones tumbled in. Where were my childhood deaf friends? What would my life have been like if I had stayed at the deaf school? How were my relationships affected by my deafness: not just my friendships but also my romantic relationships too? Eventually, I found myself confronted with the ultimate question: what was holding me back from finding, and then telling, my own story of deafness?

In making the decision to understand the impact of my deafness on my life and to answer those questions that were unsettling me, I was unsure whether to undertake my journey solo, as it were, without any guiding tools other than my memory and imagination. I wondered if it would be cheating to combine my recollections with research on deafness by experts, because although I'm deaf, I did not consider myself to be an expert. In fact, I didn't know all that much about deafness or deaf culture. I had not made it my business to make a study of it. If anything, I had made a virtue of avoiding such introspection, led by my mother's aspirations that I would live wholly as a hearing person separate from the deaf community. I did not even know many deaf people anymore. I was worried, too, that my memories would be contaminated by the influences of those other expert voices. I decided to begin my investigation at the beginning: I would return to my childhood.

2

Reunions

I found a handful of photos, stored in a plastic envelope sleeve, taken when I was a child at the Deaf School. Those photos now presented themselves as riddles to me. Every now and then I would take them out of the envelope and scatter them across my desk and look down at them, aware of the tug of nostalgia, but aware too of another feeling, a sadness of sorts, which I tried to understand each time I experienced it. I couldn't remember the little girl that I was when they were taken. I felt confronted by this absence of memory as I scanned the photos, reprising my memory's gaps across these childhood years. I felt troubled by it; discomfited by my apparent lack of loyalty to my deaf childhood, given that I seemed to remember so little of it.

Some of the photos looked as though they were snapped spontaneously; they had the blurred look of a bumped camera or lens not adjusted properly. Others had the formal composition of professional portraits, having been taken for public relations purposes to promote the Deaf School. These were taken at the bungalow-style Oral Deaf Preschool at Yeronga, a riverside suburb in Brisbane. The school pioneered an education curriculum designed to teach deaf children to speak, not through the dance of their hands, but through the effort of explosive vowels forced up through their

13

sparrow-small chests and throats, and puffy, burring, hissing consonants shaped by their tongues and lips. The photos showed teachers at work—there was Miss Clare Minchin whom I remembered as having blue stars for eyes, and there was Miss Maryanne Casey, sweet and gentle, whose wedding we attended.

The later photos were taken at the Gladstone Road School for the Deaf, which I attended after the Yeronga Preschool. Standing like a welcoming beacon on the top of a hill in Dutton Park, it was a red-brown brick Tudor-style building with mullioned windows and many rooms, set in terraced gardens and green lawns with spreading poinciana trees and Moreton Bay figs. On the grounds were swings, monkey bars, a slippery slide, and a carousel roundabout for children. Downstairs was a large area where we had dancing classes, taking our turns to balance on top of Mr. Pritchard's shiny black shoes, grasping his fingers as he glided across the floor talking to us all the while, trying to infuse in our emerging word-forced voices the motions of swinging and swelling, the tides of sound's rise and fall. Mr. Pritchard was my last teacher at the Deaf School; he went on to become a religious minister. He sketched in my brand new autograph book, in yellows and blues, the outline of a beach and sky and water and wrote about the grains of sand on the beach. It was an allegory of sorts, about God. I didn't understand the words but knew that the meaning was designed to be encouraging. Mr. Pritchard was the person who first introduced me to philosophy. He said to me, "It's what you know about yourself that matters; not what other people think." He meant that I needed to be guided by my own conscience, my own beliefs. My mother had a similar philosophy, only she called it "running your own race."

My favorite photo was a black and white class photo of the class of '62. I would have been seven years old by then. I was positioned in the middle of a group of seven children—five girls and two boys. Narelle, John, Sharon, (me, leaning forward), Kay, Colin, and Margaret. Five of us sat on a brick garden wall, our legs swinging above the ground, our hands in our laps uniformly posed, right hand resting on top of the left. The two tallest girls in the class stood sentrylike, clasping their hands, at the opposite ends of the group. We did not look directly into the camera. Instead, our eyes were turned to something or someone beyond the left border of the picture: what lay outside that left frame? The photo must have been taken in winter, because we all wore pullovers, their dark colors providing the background texture for the long looping cords of our metal-box hearing aids.

When I looked at all those photos, I felt a tenderness toward the children. Without exception, all our faces revealed undercurrents of bewilderment, as if we were aware that something was missing, but we were not sure what the missing thing was. I certainly didn't know we were missing sound, because I didn't experience the absence of hearing as a loss. My world was complete: I didn't yearn to hear; I wasn't wracked by grief or alarm or dismay because I couldn't hear; I didn't see myself as wanting or different in any way at all. I felt safe at that school where for five years, in my grey uniform with maroon trim, I was taught how to listen, to watch lips, and to talk. The more I gazed at the photos of my Deaf School days, the greater was the distance that I felt I had traveled since then. By some process of alchemy, I had been transformed from a deaf child sequestered in a school exclusively shared with other deaf children into a woman who, though still deaf, lives and works and dreams in a world in which her friends and colleagues hear sounds unaided. I wondered how this had happened, and so during a quiet moment at work one day, I pulled out the White Pages, found the numbers I was looking for, and made two telephone calls. One to Miss Casey, now Mrs. Kelly, and one to Miss Minchin.

"What was I like? Can you remember?" I asked Maryanne Kelly, the preschool teacher whom I'd known as Miss Casey, forty-two years and a lunchtime since we had seen each other. I had kept abreast of the main events in her life through the grapevine. Her mother lived around the corner from my mother; they had swapped family news over the years. I knew about Mrs. Kelly's four children and many grandchildren; she knew the vagaries of my career. Even so, I was nervous about seeing her. I didn't want to impose on her for news from another time. I had already spoken briefly on the phone with her, to organize the meeting, and she had sounded nervous too: "I'm not sure what I'll remember. What if I can't remember what you want to know?"

I had driven to her home, where we greeted each other with affection and awe, because there we were, together in her dining room overlooking Moreton Bay, after all these years. The small girl in me recognized the young teacher with the gentle smile in the still-youthful grandmother standing before me. Our conversation flowed easily, leap-frogging from topic to topic in no special order. Maryanne's curiosity meant that some of the jumps in conversation were random and unpredictable, sometimes halting me in my mind-tracks so that I could take the necessary swerve to follow her course of thinking. Her husband Tony enjoyed the occasion too, encouraging Maryanne with this story and that anecdote. "Tell about how you . . . ," he prompted her at intervals.

Several things became apparent: her dedication to her vocation; the playfulness she brought to her teaching; and her prescience in suspecting that oralism was being forced with zealotry upon deaf children, whether it was suitable for them or not. Maryanne's retelling of her teaching days revealed a strength of emotion that may have even surprised her. She remembered all our names, our hearing histories, our idiosyncrasies, our temperaments. She remembered our parents' ambitions for us. Her remembering was not only sharp and clear: it was also filled with warmth and humor, but most of all, with a continuing concern for us all. She was still worried about one little girl in particular. "Oralism wasn't suitable for her. She was just so profoundly deaf. We couldn't get the pitch of her voice down, no matter what we did. I don't know what happens to such children now. What happens to them? Oh! And the dancing lessons!" She leant toward me in laughter at that memory. It made her happy; her mood shifted. She described how much we liked to dance, to feel the vibrations of the floor boards beneath our feet as we moved up and down in time to music we could not hear.

Those days had had a big impact on her. She had not expected to be a teacher of little deaf children without language: her ambition at Teachers' College had been to teach literature to high school students. But she went where the Education Department sent her. The first few weeks were awful: "The noise! I couldn't bear the noise. All that slamming of desks and loud voices and stamping feet . . ." I reared back, my mouth agape. "I don't remember any noise at all." We looked at each other in surprise and a renewed comprehension of our different starting points. She hears, I don't.

Maryanne showed me the wedding photo of her with us, with the class of 1961, and laughed when I showed her that I'd brought the same photo with me, along with some others. She fell about at a class photo of us dressed as fairies and elves. "Just look at you!" And at the one in which my hair is cut freakishly short. "I'd cut my plaits off the day before," I explained. "That's right! That's exactly the sort of thing you did!" she laughed. Her merriment was infectious. "And what was I like?" I asked. "You! You were so vibrant! You were full of life; so keen. You just loved everything. You were just such a happy little child." She paused. "You were right out there. Everyone gathered around you. It must have been a real wrench changing schools, going from the security of a small loving group to such a big school." She looked at me; I agreed, briefly acknowledging how several years passed before I stopped missing Sharon, my best friend.

Maryanne talked about how the teachers back then basically muddled through as best as they could. They were pioneering an approach that they knew little about and for which they received only limited training or support. At the same time, they had to teach the regular academic education curriculum, sorting out for themselves how to get such information into the profoundly, severely, moderately, and mildly deaf children ranged before them. Back then, and this is possibly just as true today, the quality of children's education lay as much in the strength of their teachers' commitment toward their charges as it did in the soundness, or lack of it, in a particular educational approach. Oralism had its fans and its critics: the true believers considered it to be the only option if deaf children were to take their full place in the hearing world; the opponents regarded it variously as a form of cultural imperialism or as simply unrealistic, demanding too much of the deaf child and too much of that child's family. It eventually gave way in the late sixties to the next educational trend: "Total Communication," in which the child chose to sign, speak, or do a combination of both.

I left my meeting with Maryanne Kelly feeling overwhelmed, in tumult. I was stunned by my good luck. I was lucky to have been in the right classroom—her classroom—at the right time, and I was relieved to have been granted the opportunity to talk with her after all these years. I began to sense that the absence of hearing in my life had been, and still is, filled not just by sound, but by the love, care, and attention of many people.

I experienced this again some weeks later when I met with Miss Clare Minchin, my preschool teacher whom I had remembered as having blue stars for eyes. She met me at the front door of her home, the sounds of classical music swelling from the lounge room behind her. Age had not dimmed her: the light still shone from her eyes. She greeted me with a question, "Can you hear this music? Isn't it absolutely wonderful?" I felt the same tug of surprise that I had experienced when Maryanne described her memories of the noise of the Deaf School. My memories of Miss Minchin were limited to her teaching me the fundamentals of sound; the possibility that she enjoyed the fullness of sound in all its musicality had never occurred to me. Like Maryanne Kelly, she remembered the children in my class at the Deaf School with affection. And also like Maryanne, she conveyed a strong sense of custodianship toward her classrooms of deaf children. She was moved by the responsibility of it all: she saw the task of teaching speech as essential for the children's personal safety and needs.

But rather than talk about her memories of those days, Clare Minchin was keen to share her knowledge about oral deaf education. She explained how she had been sent to Manchester University in England by the Oral Deaf Pre-School Association in the early-to-mid-1950s to learn about the latest teaching methods. She returned to Brisbane bearing the trophy of specialist knowledge on oralism and now she wanted to transfer to me the excitement of that knowledge. She had loved teaching "the little deaf children." She was passionate about it and, even now, was still immersed in the detail of it. When I commented on Mrs. Mason's failed efforts to teach me the "ess" sound, she leapt at the opportunity to teach me anew: "Can you do an 'ess' now? Do you know what an 'ess' is? It's the thin line, the very thin air. 'Sshh' is the broad air." She took my hand, held it up to her mouth and pushed out her lips. I could feel the shirring of moist air on the back of my hand. "Well, 'ess' is the thin air." She held onto my hand, stretched her lips, and pressed together her top and bottom teeth to show me. "Thin air," she repeated. I felt the hiss on my skin and promised to practice this in front of the mirror back home.

I asked Clare why she thought I had succeeded in the oral deaf education system while some others had not. She was quick to answer. It was a question for which she knew the answer from a lifetime's vocation in teaching. "Deafness for some people doesn't impede a lot, but for some, depending on their degree of deafness and their ability to lipread, well it's harder. Yes, it's harder." She paused. "I'll give you what I think about lipreading." She pointed toward a window. "If we look outside and see a tree, and three people sit in the same position and draw what they see is the tree, they'll each draw it differently. The first one will sort of draw a stick type of tree, like a child. The next one will do better, perhaps put some leaves on it, a bit more detail. But the third one is an artist and draws it properly, draws it so you know what it looks like—unless of course he's a modernist, a Picasso! Right."

She stopped to catch her breath. She wanted to be sure that I understood her point. "So what happens with the artist is this: their eyes see, their brain tells their hands what to do, how to do it. Right. Lipreading: your eyes see to tell your brain to copy those lip movements. There's not much difference, is there? Between eyes seeing the tree and the hand drawing it, or eyes seeing the lips and the brain copying the shapes." She leant back into her chair. "But look, that's only my theory. I'm not an expert on this. Not at all. That's just my interpretation of why some deaf people have the ability to talk in the hearing world."

Clare Minchin's conceptualization of lipreading as an art rather than a science made sense. I was aware of the creativity associated with the task of lipreading. After all, I don't actually see or read every single syllable enunciated to me. I spend much energy guessing what is being said by filling in any missing information by drawing on the circumstances of the conversation. Many words have different meanings in different contexts, and I need to pick my way through this web of word trickery. My mother remembers an early childhood example of my comprehension in understanding the elasticity of words when she said to me once, "We'll have to catch a bus." I looked surprised and then scooped the air with my cupped hands, laughing "Catch a ball!" I scooped the air again, shouting, "Catch a bus!"

Clare expanded on her theory. She explained that this sense of artistry needs to be supported by a sense of confidence. Unless a deaf child feels confident enough to ask a new hearing friend to repeat what they have said, or to remind a teacher to face the classroom when they are speaking, then that deaf child is unlikely to succeed in oral integrated or mainstream education. "That's why you did well," she said. Her voice held an undercurrent of wistfulness: she wanted every deaf child to benefit from oralism just as I had done. She was a "true believer," and she saw that the hard choices made on my behalf all those years ago by my parents and by my teachers had reaped significant benefits for me throughout my life, particularly in expanding my opportunities in both education and work. Still, her insights about the artistry and confidence required to succeed in oralism sounded a warning bell: it was not suitable for every deaf child.

By one of those strokes of serendipity that happens in life every now and then, during this time—I had just had my forty-eighth birthday—I received an invitation to attend the "Class of '62" reunion of my classmates from the Deaf School. When I realized that I would not be able to attend the reunion, as I would be in England by then—having succeeded in my application for a work permit as a policy manager with Kent County Council—I arranged to have lunch with the reunion's organizer, Jennifer. We had not seen each other or even been in contact since 1962, but when we saw each other again, unaware of the private histories that had aged us, we embraced with all the warmth and affection of unbroken friendship. I gripped her shoulders, bracing my arms straight out so that I could gaze on her better. She held my gaze; I could see compassion and gentleness in her eyes. Jennifer had brought photos with her; some of them were already familiar to me, others were new. As we riffled through the photos

together, exclaiming over this person and that person—Jennifer knew who
was doing what; she had assigned for herself the role of "memory-keeper"
and knew all about their careers, marriages, children, divorces, and grief;
she'd kept in touch with all their news—I started to cry. I could not explain
to Jennifer, or to myself for that matter, my sense of having lost something
by not being a part of my childhood friends' evolving lives.

On seeing my tears, Jennifer insisted on arranging for a few of my old
Deaf School classmates to meet me for an after-work drink. Between
packing up my home and taking my other farewells with the usual round
of lunches at friends' homes and dinner celebrations in New Farm's Italian
bistros, I found a time in my diary for three days later, shortly before I left
for England. Five of us gathered at the Moray Street café, smiling at each
other, excited and awkward in our efforts to breach so many years in such
a brief splice of time: Carmel, who still sported a scar from the gash on her
forehead from falling off the monkey bars on the playground; Wayne, one
of the little boys in my preschool class but who now bore the maturity of
the senior Australian Customs officer that he was; Matthew, my first boyfriend, who carried my things for me when we were both four years old at
the Oral Deaf Preschool at Yeronga, and who had visited me at least once
almost every year for the last twenty years; and Jennifer.

We tried to chat: we wanted to share our news and our clannish excitement, but the differences in our communication styles were too great to be
breached easily or quickly. The others were able to sign to each other, but
I could not sign: I had not learned Auslan, the Australian sign language.
Our ability to comprehend speech varied markedly, so that we spoke with
one another at different speeds and different pitches and even in different
grammar (Auslan is a visual and spatial language that does not always
follow the word order of spoken English), depending on who was holding
the floor at any one time. I spent much of the hour smiling; I was happy to
be with my deaf companions. I did not feel any need to do or be anything
more than that: I just simply liked being with them.

As we parted from each other amidst promises of seeing each other
again soon, I felt the weight of difference bearing down on me. I was dif-

ferent from my deaf friends, too: they could at least communicate with each other. The psychologist's question had lodged itself in me; I could not shift it. I had returned to it over and over again, but I could not work it out. It was a complex question that could not be easily answered. I was tempted to let it go.

As it happened, a suitcase gave my quest new momentum. I had gone to my mother's home to borrow one of her suitcases for my big trip to England. She owned several: a small tartan one that you can pull along to save straining your back; a large caramel brown vinyl one with fake straps and buckles stitched on the outside; a tartan overnight shoulder bag. I burrowed around the shadowy basement room, looking for a suitable one. I was full of anticipation, looking forward to my adventure. I felt myself filling up with emotion at the prospect of new and as yet unlived stories, and I was in this mood of dreaming when my mother called out to me, "Look at this!" She sounded excited. She had stumbled across an old Globite school case: it was dark brown, cardboardy in texture, with faded green and orange stripes down one side. It was dented, old, and dusty. Looking at its surface, I sensed mysteries hidden within its archival mustiness. My mother said: "I'd forgotten about this. I've kept your old things in here," and she opened up that school case, and set free into the air all the noise, smells, and sounds of my girlhood years.

I looked down at my childhood paintings resting on what looked liked layers of rubble. My mother rummaged and pushed some things aside and held other things up for me to see. I was caught up in her excitement. There was my Grade Two catechism project book. And there was an exercise book—with the legend inscribed on the front: "The Department of Public Instruction"—from my days at the Deaf School. I riffled through the pages and could remember, could *smell*, my school days. I could smell the Clag glue, the purple dye of the Roneo stenciling machine, the plastic bowls with apples diced up in small, brown discolored pieces swimming in orange juice, and the dust of the white chalk. And I could see Mr. Pritchard standing tall at the blackboard, in front of his class of twelve children, teaching the story of Androcles and the Lion. I remembered how my very best friend, Sharon, and I had listened to Mr. Pritchard, watching him as he turned the pages of a book, and how we had sat next to each other at a long bench as we copied down this story of friendship. And there it was in my exercise pad. I wanted to dive into that Globite school case and sink into its bed of memories.

My curiosity was now alight: I wanted to know more, despite my anxiety that I would be somehow overwhelmed by new knowledge. I wanted to ration my research to protect myself from being drawn into an imagined vortex of deafness that would engulf my identity and spit it back out into the hearing world as another person altogether. Who that person would be and why I should fear her, I wasn't sure. I knew that I disliked the phrase "the deaf" with its implication of just one race, a single cultural entity. I didn't like the connotation that all people who are deaf must necessarily define themselves and their lives by the fact of their deafness. I certainly didn't define myself as a member of "the deaf community." I also bristled at the packaging of the words "the deaf" into loaded phrases such as the "predicament of the deaf," accompanied with tags such as "haunted by their isolation." I particularly resented the phrase "hearing impaired," with its violent implication that a flaw in my ears—was it a rip, a tear, a wound?— had torn right through my body.

I began reading Oliver Sacks's book *Seeing Voices*. I had bought this book several years earlier. I loved the title and was drawn to the book because of it. I had kept the book next to a miniature Rococo silver-framed photo of Jack on a shelf in my bedroom where I could see both the book and the photo readily. Months would go by, and I would not take any notice of that book, but every now and then, I would pick it up and simply look at the title, *Seeing Voices*, and contemplate its meaning for me. However, I had abandoned my first reading of it halfway through. I felt that Sacks romanticized the idea of being deaf: his book is a paean to deaf people and to sign language. He was prone to drawing larger-than-life conclusions from just a handful of anecdotes; he had a tendency to marvel at the achievements of certain deaf people with excessive incredulity. The more I read, the more uncomfortable I became. I marked the spot about halfway through the book where I gave up reading when Sacks observed:

> I had felt there was something very joyful, even Arcadian about Gallaudet and I was not surprised to hear that some of the students were occasionally reluctant to leave its warmth and seclusion and protectiveness, the cosiness of a small but complete and self-sufficient world, for the unkind and uncomprehending big world outside.

This was simply too much for me. I was irritated by his sentimentality. I was irritated by the implication that these mature, intelligent young people attending university to further their education and carve out their piece of the employment sector in the future were actually children wanting to shelter within their deaf identity. (Founded in 1864, Gallaudet University in Washington, DC, is the world's only university in which all programs and services are designed for deaf and hard of hearing students.) Of course, it is likely that many deaf people—like many hearing people—do want to hide from a difficult world. But I felt frustrated by Sacks's trivializing the cultural politics of the deaf community—he seemed to paint a naive portrait of sanctity and bliss within the world of "the deaf" in valiant opposition to a brutish hearing world. Perversely, I had to admit to a renegade pang of yearning when I read Sacks's description of Gallaudet University. I recognized the instinct for wanting to be completely at home.

When I picked Oliver Sacks's book up again with the resolve to read it from cover to cover, I had a sense of standing at the edge of a diving board, springing up and down on my toes, testing the tension of the board, flexing my muscles before stretching up, arching out, and diving headlong into and through the air, and slicing through the water below cleanly without a splash. I paused. Once I let go of whatever it was that was holding me back from this dive into my identity, I might find myself submerged in another, perhaps unwelcome, world from which I could not return. A good friend, on learning of my intention to write about my deaf life, had said, "Oh, you don't want to do that. Don't go digging around. You'll just get upset. Everything's fine." I didn't speak of it again with her. I kept my counsel.

I could not stop my quest now, even in the face of such discouragement. Talking with my Deaf School teachers and reuniting with my childhood Deaf School friends whetted my appetite to do exactly what my friend told me not to do: I wanted to dig around more. Instead of being satisfied with learning about the importance of my Deaf School education and the loyal affection of my deaf friends, I felt as if I had been given pieces of a jigsaw puzzle that I could not yet comprehend. When I packed my suitcase for England, I made space between the layers of clothes for the notebooks and cassette tapes from my interviews with Mrs. Kelly and Miss Minchin. I squeezed in the Oliver Sacks book as well. These would be my companions in England.

3

Wrong Snow

Eighteen months after those conversations with my preschool teachers and that reunion with my childhood deaf classmates, I returned home to Australia from England empty-hearted. I had settled into a nice apartment overlooking the River Medway in Rochester, enjoyed the buds of new friendships, and had muddled my way through a complicated housing policy project with Kent County Council. Paris was just a Eurostar day trip away from my front door. But despite all those signs of a promising new start in my life, I had got myself caught up in some mayhem of the heart.

It began innocuously enough. I shared an office with Seumas (not his real name) in Maidstone's County Hall building, where we fell into the habit of getting together in the cafeteria to mull over policy projects. He had curly hair that sprang out from his head in a halo of shock, and a closely shaved beard that he would stroke as if he had once lost all his hair and still could not quite believe in its return. He also had the habit of gazing directly at me when I spoke and holding his gaze longer than politeness calls for. It was unsettling and provocative. I would blush and, making a mental note to hold my nerve, try to cultivate the appearance of sangfroid in response.

Giving off the air that it was his responsibility to show England to me, Seumas took me on excursions to explore the ramparts of Dover Castle; the pathways through Sissinghurst Gardens; Ely, where its cathedral emerged from the flatness of the surrounding fens like a candle on a cake; Bath Abbey with its lengthily inscribed memorials ("died after a long and tedious illness," "a woman of mild manners . . . a graceful persuasion fell from her lips"); the shingle-seaside bleakness that is Dungeness; and the historic pubs in London's Charing Cross. I thanked him. He shrugged, "It's no hardship," and used the long car trips to pump me for details of my Australian life and to regale me with stories of the absurdities of English life. Seumas talked as if it was an opportunity to get the facts right for himself: he would talk about this historical event or that geographical feature, pause and reflect, backtrack over what he had said, and then move forward again, having made things clearer in his own mind. He thrust questions at me as if they were dueling instruments. "Do you know the difference between right and wrong snow?" No, I didn't. Seumas explained it. The hapless British Rail once blamed train delays on a fall of unusually light and powdery snow that could not be caught by the snowplows; it was the *wrong* type of snow. Seumas gave in to his unrestrained curiosity about everything. Where other people are guided by the conventions of courtesy about what is or is not polite to ask, Seumas was not. He asked me why I had come to England, was I running away from something or had I come in pursuit of an adventure? Perhaps romance, even? He was gleeful and rubbed his hands together in mock mischief. "I'll get the story out of you!"

The difference between attention and affection was not always clear-cut for me, and sometimes I let myself be seduced by very little, a kind word perhaps, or a teasing smile, maybe even just a perceptive comment. Seumas's attentiveness pushed me into that slipstream between love's illusions and life's truth. I reminded myself that we were simply work colleagues enjoying the early days of friendship, nothing more.

Not long after my arrival in England, Seumas accused me, "Are you really deaf? You don't act deaf." He leant toward me across the cafeteria table at which we were sitting to peer at me more closely, as if to reassess his vision of me, to reconfigure what he was really seeing. I was startled into a nervous laugh and asked, "What does acting deaf look like?" He blushed, cast a look to the ceiling, and then with an "in for a penny, in for a pound" attitude, he held up his hands, palms facing each other, and rotated one hand around the other, jiggling his fingers as he did so. I didn't say anything in reply. In the face of my staring silence, he pushed on, "Can't you sign? Aren't you supposed to sign?" A cartoon formed in my mind's eye: a rubbery face with cursive eyebrows and elastic cheeks, mouthing words soundlessly, supported by hands moving at chest height. I saw that I was supposed to be communication in movement, an exercise in the kinesthetics of speech. If I wasn't this, if I was, God forbid, a deaf person who speaks clearly and who conducts myself in such a way as to avoid causing too much disruption or inconvenience to others without drawing attention to myself, well then, I must surely be a fraud, a fake. I finally answered Seumas, "No." He looked uncertain. How could I call myself deaf if I could understand the spoken word and speak in reply?

In my Rochester apartment, I unpacked the tapes and notes of my conversations with Maryanne Kelly and Clare Minchin, and laid them out beside my laptop, intent once more on responding to the editor's challenge to write honestly about the impact of deafness on my life. I replayed the tapes several times, the women's Australian accents sounding loud in my Rochester apartment, and compared my handwritten notes with what I could hear on the tapes and remember in the solitude of my apartment. Perhaps it was because I was alone, but my recollections made me wistful.

Feeling mellow, I wrote my recollections of my deaf childhood determined to project a positive portrait of my life as a deaf person. I was resolute in my distaste for misery-porn in which confessional stories descend into plight and tragedy, without any particular illumination of lessons to be shared. My resolution was easy to sustain, because I regarded my professional achievements as the direct products of my oral-deaf education as well as the parental support I enjoyed, combined with my relentless capacity for work and the luck of having generous mentors throughout my career. But I put the essay away unfinished, because I did not know how to end it. The question of the impact of my deafness on my life remained unanswered.

Some time passed, and Christmas came and went too. My work at Kent County Council kept me absorbed. I also took advantage of England's many bank holiday weekends to travel in Europe in between the excursions across England with Seumas. By now, he had disclosed that he was struggling with sobriety. This rattled me, as I had been diligent in avoiding men who drank too much. I knew about the rigors of alcoholism—my father's alcoholic descent and subsequent lifelong recovery through his membership in Alcoholics Anonymous had worn a groove into the patterns of our family life—and a strain entered into our friendship. I spent more time with other friends, and filled my e-mails and postcards to home with stories about Margate's jellied eels and Derek Jarman's garden at Romney Marsh; the Manchester United fans' hymnal chant of "We only had ten men!" as they downed the Tottenham HotSpurs in a historic victory; and the virtues of wellies for tramping across the fields of Speldhurst. Whenever friends from Australia came to stay, I hosted dinner parties, filling my apartment with a mess of English and Australian voices. I loved the company of my friends and was lonely in their absence. They all shared the gift of laughter, and when I was with them, I forgot I was alone.

Then destiny dealt a swift blow. Seumas lost his erratic battle with drink with self-crucifying thoroughness, giving fresh life to the word "maelstrom." He was sacked. The hell of his alcoholic collapse struck too close to home. Despite my father's late-in-life commitment to sobriety, his alcoholism had taught me this much: steer clear. My friendship with Seumas told me otherwise: I wanted to stay close. It was Seumas who put the distance between us. My survival instincts were blunted despite the intervention of an Australian consultant in London who counseled me on detachment. He talked about the guises of love in all its variations, and used words like "miracles" and "gifts," and said things that sounded mystical and spiritual. I had never had a conversation like this before. He also said, "You have to recover yourself. You must write. Writing will be your recovery." I thought about my unfinished essay on my deaf childhood. My colleagues were chasing new jobs, my work projects were near completion, and I was homesick. So it came about that my closest friend in England, Judy, and her husband Chris, hosted a farewell dinner party—replete with dressed salmon from Deal, a Kent seaside village—at her home in Folkestone, before driving me to Gatwick Airport the following morning.

4

A Great Big Wash of Tears

Be careful what you pray for. The refrain echoed in my mind as I went about the business of rebuilding my life back home. My old public service career in Queensland held the same appeal as yesterday's leftovers. I lasted just ten days before handing in my notice. My manager was gracious, and she wished me well. "What are you going to do?" My career plans were vague, but I answered with the boldness that resilience calls for. "I'm going to write. I'll work for myself as a freelance policy analyst and write." She nodded. We both knew I was faking my courage, but even false courage creates its rewards. Work projects came my way, and a real estate agent called me about an apartment overlooking the Brisbane River. It had the feel of a tree house, perched up high in the gable of a family home. I moved there rather than put out the tenants in my own Art Deco apartment just down the road.

I returned to my pre-England routines, including my daily walk and weekly swim, and picked up the habits of old friendships as best as I could. I wasn't entirely successful. Some friends complained that I had changed in a way that they did not like, describing me as "distant." Despite their entreaties, I remained reluctant to talk about the final weeks of my time in England. This was difficult territory to negotiate, because despite my grief for Seumas, I valued all that I had experienced during my eighteen months in England, but I couldn't find the right words to explain this to myself, let alone to anyone else. I still struggle, all this time later. I fell out of favor with a couple of people who lost patience with my reticence, but my closest friends stayed the course with me. They fed me, asked occasional questions, tolerated my confusion, and took me to my favorite holiday retreat on Stradbroke Island, where we swam in a sea inhabited by ancient turtles. My mother sat with me many times over several weeks, tapping her fingers on the chair, before she finally asked, "What on earth *happened*?" Her question tore more tears from me, provoking her to comment, "You don't have much luck with men, do you?" My tears dried up in a wheeze of outrage, but before I could defend myself, she ruminated, "Never mind, I've never had much luck either." Given that she had been married for forty-seven years to my father until his death eight years earlier, and was by then eighty years old with nine grandchildren and two great-grandchildren, I looked askance at her.

In between times, I wrote. I had finished my essay on deafness, "I Hear with My Eyes," and given it to a prospective publisher. In this essay, I wrote about my enthusiasm for my childhood deaf friends and recounted what my teachers had told me. I also wrote about my mother's persistence in making sure that I learned to communicate by speaking rather than signing. I crafted a selection of anecdotes, ranging in tone, I hoped, from sad to tender to laugh-out-loud funny. I speculated on the meaning of certain incidents in defining who I am and the successes I had enjoyed as a deaf woman in a hearing world. I searched carefully for what I wanted to say and concluded my essay with the words "I can listen, speak and communicate . . . precious gifts sown in my life when I was just a child." While I believed in the truth of these words and still do, I was also aware that by ending the essay in this way, I had not taken the opportunity to tackle the status quo of deaf people's standing in the world. Somehow, I had implied that it was better to be deaf and to speak than not, but I had not sufficiently explained why I believed this or even challenged why this should be so. I sat on my discomfort and hoped it would go away. I told myself it was not important.

While I waited for the publisher's reply, I wrote about other things. I wrote about my hopes in my diary as soon as I woke up in the mornings. I wrote outlines for novels after breakfast and before I started work for the day. I wrote letters and sent e-mails to friends when I should have been working. I wrote poems in the late afternoons and public policy papers for clients in the evenings with a glass of wine for company, losing track of time only to discover its passing when hunger pangs struck too late at night for me to be bothered to prepare a decent meal. My reading habits changed. Instead of turning to novels for comfort and consolation, I turned to books on love, religion, and meditation. I reread Thomas Merton's *The Seven Storey Mountain*; discovered Thich Nhat Hanh, the Buddhist monk and activist; scrolled addictively through Amazon online for reviews of new books; and used the back of art postcards to copy sentences by other writers exhorting readers to find fresh ways to see their world. I just about knocked myself out, I was in such a mania of self-improvement, intent on changing myself so I could change my life.

Falling under the thrall of seeing meaning where there is none, Seumas's story about wrong snow struck me as an apt metaphor for my own approach to life. At the time, I assumed that the reason I was not in a romantic relationship was that something must be wrong with *me*, not because of wrong men, unlucky circumstances, or bad timing. I didn't consider the possibility that that's just the way things turn out for some of us. Most of the time, I did not seriously think my being deaf was the reason I was not in a romantic relationship, but every now and then, the question would stray into the periphery of my consciousness: maybe it *was* the reason? In any case, I was resolute: I had to change something in my life, whatever that "something" might be, and I wanted to learn how to do this.

Women who become pregnant for the first time often comment that their whole world suddenly appears to be full of pregnant women. They had not noticed them before, but now, here they were, all around them. Their individual experience was not unique at all. I experienced a similar insight on completing my essay on deafness. Suddenly, every newspaper seemed to be full of stories about deafness, hearing loss, deaf culture, deaf children, and cochlear implants. Advertisements about hearing aids caught my eye, especially the annoying ones touting the virtues of "invisible" hearing aids. One newspaper article about a center for deaf children in a leafy suburb of Brisbane finally stirred me into action, and I arranged a meeting with the center's clinical director. She was a small person with large energy; her passion was bracing. Ever quick to assert the power of cochlear implants, she asked me, "Have you considered having an implant?" I said no, that I doubted I would be a suitable candidate. She gazed at me for a few moments and pronounced, "I'm sure you'd benefit from it." Her authority was compelling. I agreed to consider it.

Having won this concession from me, she walked me into a sunny room crowded with a mess of little boys and girls, all arrayed in a democracy of shorts, shirts, and sandals. Mothers and fathers, their young faces stretched with tension, stood or sat around the room's perimeter watching their children. The noise in the room was orchestral, rising and falling to a mash of shouts, cries, and squeals. A table had been set with an abundance of plastic plates in which diced pieces of browning apple, orange slices, and melon chunks swam in a pond of juice. Children clustered around it, waiting to be served, bringing to life one of my childhood photographs. I redirected my attention to the director, who introduced me to a couple of the mothers. They smiled at me in a friendly but uncertain way. I smiled back, wondering what to say. They volunteered information about their children, describing their hearing history before slipping into portraits of their personality. I murmured encouragingly in reply. When the little ones finished their morning fruit, they were rounded up to sit cross-legged at the front of the room, before a teacher poised with finger puppets of ducks. I pulled up a red plastic chair, its tiny size designed to accommodate a child's bottom, and lowered myself onto it to watch the proceedings. The boys and girls leaned forward in laughter as they watched their teacher perform the story of a mother duck and her five baby ducks. Her hands moved in a flurry of duck-billed mimicry. "'Quack! Quack! Quack!' said the mother duck!" The parents trilled along in time with the teacher.

During my drive back home, I realized I was speeding. Not just the car; my heart too. My heart seemed to be wired to the engine of the car, both racing to convince those parents to enjoy great hopes for their children.

A year later, when my essay "I Hear with My Eyes" was published in a national journal, I was pleased to see it in print and felt a sense of achievement. I had done the necessary self-reflection, and said what needed to be said. The deed was done, and I could move on to other matters. I was unprepared for the impact of the readers' responses to my essay, and by the tumble of questions put to me by parents of deaf children.

Some people said they liked my candor. Others said that they were moved by it. Friends were curious and fascinated to get the inside story of my life as a deaf person, as it had not been a topic of conversation among us. They felt that they had learned something about what it means to be deaf. Many responses to my essay and public presentations had relief and surprise as their emotional core. Parents cried on hearing me talk about the fullness of my life and seemed to regard me as having given them permission to hope for their own deaf children. Educators invited me to speak at parent education evenings because, as one of them wrote, "To have an adult who has a hearing impairment and who has developed great spoken language and is able to communicate in the community at large—that would be a great encouragement and inspiration for our families."

Leaving aside the circus-freak overtones of this particular comment, I was uncomfortable about these responses, because I was not sure that I had been as honest or direct as I could have been. What lessons on being deaf had people absorbed by reading my essay and listening to my presentations? I had not set out to be duplicitous, but had I embraced the writer's aim for the neatly curved narrative arc at the cost of the cool self-regarding eye and the uncertain conclusion?

In my essay, I had ignored the historic context of being born deaf at a time, in the mid 1950s, when people still spoke of the "pitiful deaf-mute" and the "deaf and dumb." I had downplayed the fact that I belonged to a category of children who attracted the gaze of the curious, the kind, and the cruel with mixed results, and who were bombarded with questions that we either could not hear and so could not answer, or could hear and made us shrivel in our loss of dignity. I had not drawn attention to the fact we were the patronized beneficiaries of charitable picnics organized for "the disadvantaged and the handicapped." We were also the subject of taunts, with words such as "spastic" speared toward us, as if to be called such a name was a bad thing. I could not claim innocence as my defense. I knew I had glossed over things but thought this was right and proper: why stir up jagged memories? Aren't some things better left unexpressed? Besides, keep the conversation nice, I thought.

I had also rejected the mythologizing of deafness. I had wanted my story to be free of dramatic conflict, of the pendulum swings of emotion. I wanted to be persuasive in the telling of my life as a deaf girl/deaf woman as a regular life. I knew that I stood accused of being disingenuous because my life *has* been different—and, to tell the truth, quite interesting—because of my deafness. A small part of me quite liked the romanticizing of deafness, and who wanted to be plain old ordinary? But this was mischievous of me. The reality was that I had worked very hard to be "ordinary" so that I could enjoy my place in the hearing world with my advanced education, my career, my friendships, and my relationships. I also understood my life to have been shaped by the influences of many people, events, and circumstances, and not just by the fact of being deaf. These influences—for example, my Catholicism, my convent school education, the city in which I grew up, my work—were like the interconnecting threads of a children's string game, cat's cradle. It was not possible to isolate one thread without damaging or distorting the pattern of the cradle. I felt challenged as I tried to make sense of the mix of memories, imagined scenes, inherited stories, and personal values about what matters and what doesn't, to understand the rightness or otherwise of the psychologist's question, "Your deafness, it must have had a big impact on you?"

The combination of grief and hope in readers' responses to my published essay was provocative. I was especially shocked by the intensity of so many parents' grief about their children's deafness, and frustrated by the notion that I was an inspiration because I am deaf but also oral. I wondered what this implied about my childhood deaf friends who did not speak orally as well as I do, but who nevertheless enjoyed fulfilling lives. I was chilled by the admission of a mother of a six-year-old deaf son who could not speak and had not yet been taught how to Sign. This mother, a doctor, said, "Now that I've met you, I'm not so frightened of deaf people anymore." Her small boy stood next to her, uncomprehending, his head bowed and his arms limp by his side. Her face was alive with the thrill of revelation. She seemed blind to my horror; surely my face must have shown how appalled I was? My shock may strike the average hearing person as naïve, but I was unnerved that so many parents of children newly diagnosed with deafness were grasping my words with the relief of people who have long ago lost hope for their deaf sons and daughters.

My shock was not directed at these parents but at an apparently unabated prejudice. What was going on out there in the big world that, five decades after my mother experienced her own grief, bewilderment, anxiety, and quest to forge a good life for her little deaf daughter, contemporary parents were still experiencing those very same fears and asking the same questions? Why did parents still receive the news of their child's deafness as a death sentence of sorts, the death of hope and prospects for their child, when the facts show that far from being a death sentence, the diagnosis of deafness propels a child into a different life, not a lesser life? Evidently, a different sort of silence had been created over the years; not the silence of hearing loss but the silence of lost stories, invisible stories, unspoken stories.

I had contributed to that silence. More than that, I *authored* it. My very silence about my deafness *was* my story. But it had acted as a brake of sorts. I had, for too long, buried the chance to better understand the complex lives of deaf people as we negotiate the claims and demands of the hearing world. For as long as I could remember, and certainly for all of my adult life, I was careful to avoid being identified as "a deaf person." Although much of my career was taken up with considering the rights of people with a disability, I had never advocated specifically for deaf people or deaf rights. Some of my early silence about deaf identity politics was consistent with my desire not to shine the spotlight on myself in this way. I did not want to draw attention to myself just because I had less hearing than other people. I had thought that if I lived my life as fully as possible in the hearing world and with as little fuss as possible, then my success in blending in would be eloquence enough. If I was going to attract attention, I wanted it to be on the basis of merit, on what I achieved. Others would draw the necessary conclusion that deaf people can take their place fully in the hearing world. My silence became a habit, and like so many enduring habits, it did not always sit comfortably with me. I was compromising myself in a way I could not quite grasp.

Now I looked around me and wondered, "Why don't I bump into more deaf people during the course of my daily life?" I was not a recluse. I had traveled down the eastern seaboard of Australia, across Europe and to New York, and had worked in a public policy career for thirty years, scaling the competitive ladder with a reasonable degree of nimbleness. Such a career had got me out and about quite a bit, and yet not once in those thirty years did I get to share an office or a chance meeting or a lunch break with another deaf person. The one exception that proved the rule was my meeting in England with James Strachan, a profoundly deaf, charismatic man, and about whom I will write in a later chapter.

My certainty about what I'd claimed in that essay wobbled: *I* wobbled. I wondered who I was.

The financial strain of working for myself, the corrosiveness of my disappointment in love, and the burden of my resentful fear at the prospect of being single for the rest of my days coalesced into the question "What's the point of it all?" It was too much. Two telephone conversations saved me from despair.

The first one took place shortly after I made a mad dash from Australia to London (a twenty-six-hour flight, economy class) and back home again within five days. I had not cut my ties with England. If anything, my friendships with my English friends had strengthened with a diet of telephone calls and e-mails about their lives in Speldhurst, Tonbridge, Folkestone, Somerset, and London. Seumas was keeping me posted about his efforts to pull himself together through an addiction recovery program, and Judy had come out for a holiday, persuading me to show her off to my Australian friends with a round of dinner parties and visits to my favorite beaches at Noosa, Byron, and Stradbroke. When I was invited to attend a job interview with the UK Design Council in London, it presented itself as a chance to start over again in England. I was equivocal, I wasn't really enthusiastic; it would mean another upheaval, but on the other hand, I didn't feel strong enough to say no to such an invitation. As it turned out, I was not offered the job after all. The whole exercise took its toll.

An old school friend, Maria, heard the exhaustion in my voice on the telephone just a day after my return from London. Her response was instantaneous. "You must go on a retreat." She gave me the details, and I did just that. At the Bethel healing retreat, run by two former nuns in a hillside house that tilted into its aging, papery timbers as it overlooked the sea, I learned a little more about the compassion of love. I came to understand that the teacher I was looking for in my life lay within me. I was also shown how to meditate.

The second telephone conversation took place a few months later. It was Easter Monday, but it was the most un-Easterly of all Easters for me. I had another work deadline to meet and more real estate agents to call; I had sold my New Farm home and was in search of a new home by the river. It did not feel like a feast day at all. It was just another public holiday. Just another day. I sank into a deep melancholy, was immobilized by it. I tried to sleep it off but was too wide awake. I made an effort to distract myself with work but could not settle. I turned my attention to a new essay on deafness written by a colleague, whereupon I fell into a great big wash of tears. In the essay, my colleague had recounted a deaf teenage boy's experience: he was successful in all that he did but he nevertheless succumbed to depression and attempted to kill himself; he survived his own attack to reveal that he was very lonely; he did not know any other deaf people and had never met any deaf adults; he had taken this to mean that deaf people die young.

I cried as if I had never cried before. The boy's story was inside me. It bumped up against the psychologist's question—"Your hearing loss must have had a big impact on you?"—which hummed like radio echo waves beneath the surface of my daily activities and nightly dreams. I lay down on the floor, my head on a pillow, with the aim of quietening myself by meditating. Closing my eyes, I breathed in time to my tears and eventually my tears subsided, and my breath was more even. I watched the vivid red-scarlet colors behind my closed eyes for a long time and kept watching as the red transformed itself into purple, like a red roof sliding back to reveal a purple sky. Peace settled in me. I kept still. As I lay there, on the prickly carpet, taking in the purple colors, the name of a friend whom I had not seen for too long bubbled up into my mind. Maryanne.

We had known each other years ago. She had long black hair falling down to her waist, and she liked to promote herself as a hippie, but despite her zany take on life, she was, at heart, too solid to be a real hippie. At first, our friendship was based on the light ease of mutual friends, conversations about books, and gossip. Then, our affection deepened when Jack died; we shared a bond of grief, as both of us lost babies too young. Over the years, I had drawn on her older wisdom; still did, despite her physical absence; "Love is always close to you," she liked to tell me. She lived now with her husband in the northern rivers area of New South Wales, where she wrote and he painted. Maryanne. I had been meaning to telephone her to get news of a mutual friend, Louise, in Canada. Now was the time to call her again.

"What's up, sweetheart?" She came straight to the point when she heard the tears in my voice. "Is it Jack?" "No, not this time." We spoke of our babies for a few minutes—their presence remained strong for each of us—before I answered her opening question, "No, it's as if I've got empty-nest syndrome. I've worked so very hard all these years to cope with my sadness, to keep busy, but now it's time for me to stop working so hard. It's time for me to live my life differently, but I'm finding it very difficult even though I know I must." Maryanne murmured humming-like sounds in a series of sustained breaths while I said these words. She didn't say anything. I kept going. "I've been thinking. I've been wondering." I stopped. I could not say the words that were in my chest. "Yes, sweetheart? You've been wondering?"

I pushed on. "Well, sometimes I think that my happiest days were when I was at the Deaf School," and I could not say anything more. I breathed heavily. Maryanne waited at the other end of the line. I gulped air and expelled it in the question, "I wonder if I feel so lonely because I don't have any deaf people in my life?" I wasn't precisely sure what I meant by this question, given that I had my childhood deaf friends I could call upon, but the absence of their routine presence in my adult life seemed wide and gaping. Maryanne erupted. "I *love* this!" she sang. "This is just so exciting!" She cried out in exclamation marks in her excitement. "You are on the right track! You know you are!" And I *did* know.

PART TWO

5

Talk Speak Words Sign

Some months later, I signed up for Auslan classes. At the end of the first lesson one summer evening, I rang my sister.

"You'll never guess what I've just done."

"No."

I stood in my kitchen, phone in hand, and watched steam rising from the kettle. My face felt hot, at odds with the cold tension settling into my jaw.

"I've just been to an Auslan class. You know, Australian sign language."

"Godalmighty," Cecily's alarm barreled down the telephone line. "Don't tell Mum. It'll kill her."

"Don't say that. Don't even joke about it."

"I'm not."

My heart hammered as I reached for the kettle before the water boiled over.

The following Saturday, I told my niece Jess. She looked into the dregs of her coffee. A waitress in a blur of white and black flounced by us. "Well?" I prompted.

Jess chewed the inside of her cheek and then smiled. "Won't Grandma guess when you start slipping into the occasional sign? That's not going to be too good for you, is it?"

Most deaf children are born into hearing families who have little contact with other deaf people. The hearing families' understanding of deafness is usually slight and may also be contaminated by dimly recalled caricatures of deaf people and deafness in old books or films. Despite their own children being deaf, they do not routinely witness the lives of other deaf people, and nor do they generally seek out—either for themselves or for their children—documented stories, fiction or biographical, of deaf people's lives. They rely on the rare accidental brush with a deaf adult, their children's school environment, and conversations with other parents as their main sources of guidance, knowledge, and hopes about their deaf child's prospects. This not only has implications for how the hearing family members regard the deaf child but also for how the deaf child regards herself. The hearing parents—and perhaps the siblings too—want the deaf child to be *normal*, to *fit in*.

Such was the power of oralism in my family that the very idea of learning Australian sign language throbbed with the potency of sin. Many sins. Sloth. Exhibitionism. Forming cabals. Deaf people who signed did not work hard enough at talking. They drew attention to themselves. Worse still, they gathered together in tight communities, isolated from the rest of the world. For these sins, there was no forgiveness through penance; instead, the penalty of banishment from the "normal" hearing world was the unvoiced threat. Not just for me, but for all my family. Cecily demanded, "You must remember! None of us was allowed to learn the deaf person's alphabet. Mum tore the pages out of the back of the encyclopedia so that we couldn't learn it."

No matter that I had a lifetime of speaking aloud etched into my history, and that I was not seeking to be absorbed into the Deaf-signing community. Besides, wasn't I the poster girl for oralism? A 1960 television magazine had reported my mother's claim that I was "a new person through lipreading." She said, "The 'live' TV commercial enables Donna to follow what is being said without being able to hear any spoken words." This might have been so, but my mother went on to stretch credulity: "She has become an avid TV fan as a result of this and can sing the entire theme of the *Mickey Mouse Club* from beginning to end." I was barely five years old. And now here I was, nearly fifty years later, sitting through my first Auslan class at the center for Deaf Services Queensland (having parked my car in the adjacent church car park) feeling as though all the security cameras in the world were trained on me: caught! Each week for ten weeks, I attended those Auslan classes bristling with the frisson of extreme risk, and worried about doing my homework too diligently. What if I started backsliding in my spoken speech? What if I woke up one morning entirely mute and resistant to verbal communication? What if I *signed*?

Most children are curious about where they come from. Such curiosity marks their first foray into their sexual development and sense of identity. I do not remember expressing such curiosity; it congealed, instead, around stories of my deafness. I seemed to be marked by two birth events, with the diagnosis of my deafness heralding my real arrival, overriding the false start of my physical birth three years earlier. My mother said that once she realized I was deaf, she was able to get on with it, the "it" being to defy the odds of a constrained life for her deaf child. She came out swinging. By hook or by crook, her deaf daughter was going to learn to speak and to be educated and to take her place in the hearing world and to live a normal life and that was that.

I grew up with the notion that my mother had been shocked into the realization that I was deaf during Guy Fawkes festivities one hot November when the night sky had exploded with the flashlights and noise of fireworks, and young children had cried in fright, and I had contentedly sucked my fingers. But in the course of writing this book, I learned that while this incident took place, it was not the trigger of discovery. "No," my mother said, "No, I'd been worried for a long time because you weren't speaking." She had mentioned her concerns several times over a period of many months to her doctor, a man whom she regarded as a friend and so trusted completely, but this doctor assured her. "Everything's fine," he said. "Don't worry." But my mother did worry. She traipsed around town from specialist to specialist; why wasn't I talking like my older sister and brother? Once or twice, she was told that I was mentally handicapped or just slow, but she knew with all the sureness of a mother's heart that this was simply wrong. It didn't fit with what she saw in me each day: my alertness, and my ability to read her moods and my world from the most subtle cues. My mother was defiant about this: once, a woman on a tram recoiled from me and asked, "Is she retarded?" Mum snapped back, "No. Are you?" Her eyes dared the woman, a stranger to her, to speak again.

My mother took to watching me closely, saw my own watchfulness, and wondered about that. One day, as she pegged some washing to dry on the clothes line, with me playing around her feet, she dropped a peg from the laundry basket onto the lawn, stood still with her hands by her sides, and said, "Donna, pick up the peg." Nothing. No reaction. But when she pointed to the peg, I hurried over to pick it up for her, and put it in her outstretched hand. Another time, she stood at the kitchen doorway and called out, "We're going to the shops now." Again, nothing, but as she walked toward me with her handbag, I stirred with excitement: we were going shopping! Then there was the bath towel test: she sang out that it was time for my bath; I ignored her; she walked over to me trailing a bath towel by her side and I ran happily to the bath. In this way, my mother gathered her data and reached her own conclusion: my eyes were doing the work of my ears. I knew how to comprehend my world, but I couldn't hear and I couldn't speak. Time must have stalled for my mother; she must have felt suspended between disbelief and clarity; she dithered. A good friend of hers, Mrs. Hackett, finally set time rolling again when she blurted out one hot December day, "Did you know that your Donna's deaf?" Overwhelmed by what she had just said, Mrs. Hackett cried, wanted to take back her words, but my mother said that this was the jolt she needed. She was not being neurotic; something *was* wrong with her youngest child, and something needed to be done. Now.

She made an appointment with the Commonwealth Acoustics Laboratory housed in a sandstone building next to Anzac Square in Brisbane's Adelaide Street. Some of the questions puzzled her. "Can Donna drink through a straw? How does she walk up the stairs, bilaterally or does she put forward the same foot each time, and steady herself on each step before proceeding?" My mother reported that yes, I could drink through a straw, but that as a matter of fact I did walk up the stairs awkwardly. In addition to these questions—my mother still doesn't understand their purpose or what her answers revealed about me—the audiologist put headphones on me and made sounds for a while. He showed my mother how the dots and crosses on the hearing assessment graph were in the wrong squares, much too low down on the page. The downward sloping lines connecting these pencil marks on the graph meant that I could hear deep-pitched trumpet-like sounds directly channeled into my ear, but not the high-pitched ones, neither the murmur of conversation nor the call of birds.

At the next appointment, I was fitted with a hearing aid. By 1957, hearing aid technology had advanced since the first editions of the "wearable hearing aid," which consisted of a black transmitter with two cords, one connected to the earpiece and the other to the battery, which was worn separately, strapped to the thigh. Mine was a compact transistor-like box about the size of a square drink coaster and just thick enough to hold an AA battery, with a pink plastic-coated cord linking it to the earpiece. I wore my metal box in a light cotton harness underneath my clothes for fifteen years. An instrument for piercing silence, it absorbed and conveyed sounds, with those sounds eventually separating themselves out into patterns of words and finally into strings of sentences. Through the fog of learning how to watch, listen, and speak over the next several years, I saw, heard, and said its name as "hirrinayde." When I switched my metal box on, I was switched on, and when I switched it off, well then, *I* was switched off. It was just another piece of clothing. I was nine years old before I realized what the words were—"hearing aid"—and absorbed their meaning as being something to help me hear. I was simultaneously surprised and embarrassed. Surprised because I did not understand myself as someone who required help to hear; I was deaf, certainly; that much I understood. Embarrassed because, of course, I *did* need help to hear; how could I not have understood that material fact earlier?

My mother's heart must surely have stopped, for a juddering split second, when she heard the words lodged deep within her, waiting to be released by the cool voice of a professional, "Your daughter is deaf." She yielded up this diagnosis to my father back home. How carefully my mother must have chosen words designed not to fracture her husband's dreams—or would they have been fears?—for his little girl. She would have wanted her words to act as a trajectory of hope. All the same, my father reacted "very poorly," mum said. The corners of her mouth tightened: she was wry in her assessment. "He put his pork-pie hat on his head and just went out. He found a reason to go out every night, what with his meetings with this club and that association. He manufactured any excuse at all not to be around so that he didn't have to talk about it. He kept it up for about six to eight months." She was matter-of-fact about this, simply raising an eyebrow. "Oh, you know how it is. Men don't like to think there's anything wrong with their children. They think it reflects badly on them." After a while, my father joined an association of parents who raised funds to set up the Oral Preschool for the Deaf at Yeronga.

The push for this school resulted from a visit to Australia in the early 1950s by two leaders of British oralism, Sir Alexander and Lady Irene Ewing from Manchester in the United Kingdom. They advocated early diagnosis and early educational support so that deaf children could communicate in the hearing world by using spoken language. I was among the first intake of children in the year it opened, 1957.

I learned more about this history while I was writing this memoir, when I visited my old preschool and spent several hours hunched over large photograph albums covered in off-cuts of wallpaper. A lawn mower growled in a nearby garden; I turned my hearing aids off. Page after page of those albums was pasted with clippings from newspapers and photographs from the 1950s and 1960s. They showed how mothers and fathers campaigned for the best education for their deaf children—and the sooner, the better.

One little deaf girl's face peered out of several photos; I recognized her expression of "What's going on?" as mine. I put names to the faces of the other children, pressing a finger down in genuflection on their images at each trip of my memory wire. There was Norman and there was Wayne, and here was Kay, and there was Jennifer, and here again, Matthew and Sharon. Oh! and there was a photo of my mother! How young she looked back then, with her wavy dark hair and dressed in her slim-line linen suit.

In the fading afternoon light, I turned my attention to the crumbly stacks of meeting minutes and administration files stained nicotine-yellow with age. One or two pages crackled beneath the weight of turning. Much work had been done on the parents association's constitution; words had been penciled in by hand over typed words, and pieces of paper were taped here and there to replace old text with new. The membership list of the parents' association recorded the men's names—Mr. J. N. Nicholson, Mr. I. Perry, Mr. J. Kinnane, and so on—together with their occupations as clerks, truck drivers, accountants, sales managers, and a physiotherapist. Their wives' names and occupations were not listed. My mother's name was an exception: she was recorded as the honorary treasurer of the Women's Pre-School Auxiliary and my father was the treasurer of the Pre-School Association. Minutes of meetings were endorsed by the loop and swirl of my father's signature. One meeting reported my father's visit to Parliament House in George Street, Brisbane, to lobby the politicians. It included a transcript of his interview with Radio 4BK's "Getting to Know You" program on December 28, 1958. The interviewer asked, apparently in some anguish, "But surely something can be done medically to cure their deafness?" My father answered, "I'm afraid there are no Christmas bells for deaf children, Mr. Kiley."

Long after the new preschool was established, the parents continued to fight ignorance and bureaucracy. For several years, the Queensland Government, which maintained the School for the Deaf, Dumb and Blind in Annerley, opposed the existence of the new oral preschool in the neighboring suburb. I read a clipping from a 1959 morning newspaper, which reported the claims of a public servant who said it was sufficient to "give

deaf children an education favourably comparable with that of the ordinary primary school." He said there was no need to go further than grade
eight, as most deaf children did four or five years of manual training or
domestic science. Imagine it. In 1959, Soviet Russia crash-landed Luna 2
onto the moon as the first man-made object; the United States launched
the first weather station into orbit and took the first pictures of Earth from
space; but back in Australia, an education bureaucrat said it was unrealistic
for deaf students to aspire to catch the cross-river ferry to the University
of Queensland, where they might study to be a veterinary surgeon, social
worker, teacher, engineer, lawyer, or doctor. In the face of such lassitude, the
parents' ambitions for their deaf children must have been stoked by anger,
as well as fear and frustration.

Finally, I found the visitors' book, a black folder with ruled lines marking
out rows and columns. My parents' signatures, dated July 28, 1957, were
inscribed one beneath the other—*James Albert* in Queensland-convent
copperplate script, nine lines from the top of the page, and *Eloise Helen*
in cramped New South Wales cursive style, seven lines further down the
page. I traced my fingers over the lines of ink and felt the pulse of my parents' long-ago hopes goose-bumping my skin. I imagined how my parents
would have queued up to the table with the visitors' book, impatient to sign
their names, as if by their signatures alone, they would put their stamp on
my education, on my life: I would speak and I would learn. I closed my eyes
and breathed in and out deeply for a few moments, nursing the book on
my lap. When I opened my eyes again, as if surfacing from a dream, I felt
the push and pull of love's tides across all my nights and days. Any loneliness I felt was simply the twin to love, each in orbit to the other. I shut
the visitors' book, put everything back in the cupboards, looked around the
room one last time, and turned my hearing aids back on before walking out
into the late afternoon air.

My sister and brother were only children themselves—eight and six
years respectively—when they first took on the news of their three-year-
old sister's deafness. They learned they had to face me when they spoke
to me. They watched my mother as she taught me about the purpose-

fulness of sounds, as she pressed my hand against her lips so I could feel the expulsion of air shaping letters, and as she splayed my fingers against the pulsing of words bubbling up her throat. They transformed themselves into word-mirrors for me: with their cupid-mouths stretched, they shaped and reshaped sounds for me to see. Some sounds were beyond my reach; some shapes held more than one meaning: to my eyes, "yellow balloon" was "lello balloon," the "y" and the "l" looking the same on people's lips. My sister, Cecily, remembers having to adopt new routines intended to establish conversation with me. She explained, "We had to say, 'Good morning, Donna. How are you today?' and you had to say, 'Good morning, Cecily. I'm very well, thank you.' The only problem was that sometimes I would say something else, like 'Good morning, Donna, you stink!' and you would still try to say your words." Innocent to my difference, I reflected back to my family an image capable of being shaped by their love and attention and, evidently, occasional teasing. Without knowledge, without speech, and immersed in my world of visual, tactile, and intuitive but noiseless senses, I was coaxed, dragooned, and persuaded into the world of hearing, a world of bubbles, balloons, and fingers placed on lips to learn the shape, taste, and feel of sounds, their push and pull of air through tongue and lips.

I remember some of these things clearly, but other memories are more like a pulse, a humming beat of a song that I can't quite catch. My memories are not whole, just fragments of images, whiffs of smells. I don't remember any sounds from my early childhood days at all. I don't remember squeals of happiness, or the sounds of my teachers' voices, or the rabble of the playground. I don't remember tidbits of eavesdropped conversations, or fairy tales whispered in singsong lilts to me at night. I don't remember any of this because I didn't experience it in the first place. Instead, my aural memory is one of quiet, as if I had lived in a chamber of silence. Not total silence: more like muffledness, as if a heavy blanket was thrown over all the sounds of my childhood.

Each Tuesday evening, as I pushed open the door to the Auslan class, I held hopes of discovering something new about my deaf history. I was filled with a sense of adventure, and thought that the act of learning the mechanics and culture of sign language would help me to better understand my own relationship to my deafness, especially given its influence on other people's perceptions of what it means to be deaf. On the first night, I discovered that my Auslan teacher for the term was going to be Jennifer, the same Jennifer who had sought me out a few years earlier to arrange the reunion with my deaf school friends. We hugged each other and laughed before settling into the protocols of the teacher-student relationship. She stood at the front of a whiteboard, and I joined the other students seated around her in a ragged semicircle of chairs.

Jennifer handed out sheets of paper with stamp-sized pictograms of hands mobilized in the shapes of the Auslan alphabet and some commonly used words, phrases, greetings, and questions, and then asked each of us to say why we wanted to learn this language of hand signs. An interpreter, a young man with a husky voice, sat with us and spoke aloud the words that Jennifer signed. It was odd, at first, to hear a man's voice transcribing her words. As the students gave their reasons in voices of varying pitch, confidence, and age, the interpreter silently signed and mouthed their words back to Jennifer. One boy, who looked to be just seventeen years old and wore the boots of an apprentice, said that he wanted to get to know a deaf girl he'd met at a dance recently; a Greek man in his twenties flushed as he explained that he had just become an uncle, his newborn nephew was deaf, and he wanted to participate fully in his nephew's life; two young women with swinging blonde hair and dressed in the smart navy pleated skirts and crisp white shirts of a travel agency said their deaf customers had difficulty communicating with them and so they planned to become fluent in Auslan and develop a niche market providing a travel service for deaf people; and a third girl's voice bubbled with her excitement, "I've always wanted to learn a second language!" Her brother bobbed his head, "Me too!"

I was the only deaf student in that class of twelve, and the others were fascinated to discover the existence of a deaf person who could not sign. Their exclamations of "Why not?" crashed into their incredulity, "You speak so well!" and into their curiosity, "Why are *you* learning Auslan?" I kept my answer simple; I said that I wanted to be able to speak with my old classmates from the Deaf School, and had vague ideas of seeking them out. It was a threadbare answer. I was embarrassed by the truth. My deafness didn't automatically mean that I was empathetic about other people's difficulties. I was as guilty as anyone else in my lack of imagination about the individual stories that lie within each of us. This was despite the insistence of others that I must be the holder of certain values, as someone who is sensitive to "these sorts of things" simply because I was deaf. I was just a small child, playing with friends at a neighbor's home down the road, when I was first made aware of this. We had crowded around the kitchen table, waiting for a batch of newly baked cupcakes to cool so that they could be coated with sugary pink and white icing. As we fidgeted and jostled, one of the children told a long-winded joke which finally ended with the punch line of a person with spastic hand movements inadvertently jerking a cone of ice cream into his face. I had long lost track of the story but as everyone in the room laughed, I smiled too. Then the joke-telling child went red-faced, flicked a look at me, and mumbled, "Sorry, I know you don't like that sort of thing." Her deference was unwarranted; after all, my childhood deaf friends and I were unsympathetic toward the blind children at the Deaf and Blind School where we would go for the annual sports day. We didn't like playing with them. My sister recalls those Deaf and Blind School sports days: "The blind kids would run to the bell and the deaf kids didn't even know it was being rung." Their expressionless faces with eyes turned skyward instead of toward the horizon ahead and their uncoordinated walking unsettled me. I felt uneasy about the blankness of their faces with their soft open mouths; I didn't want to bump into them as they weaved their way across the sports field. And, as I've just realized with a guilty jolt while writing this, my deaf friends and I would have complained in our loud unleashed voices about those little blind children, completely unmindful that they could, of course, hear us.

The thing is, I have always hated the stereotype "If deaf, *ergo*, must then sign." I resented the implication that if I did not sign, then I must not really be deaf, or worse still, that I had no right to identify myself as deaf.

I had had so little contact with other deaf people since my childhood that I could not understand why they would choose to sign. I knew about the mortification of self-consciousness—I cannot make the sound "ess," and I can still see, with chest-burning sickness, the contorted spittle-spoiled mouth of the nun who mimicked my efforts as a fourteen-year-old girl trying to say the word "scissors," thus sentencing me to forever act out the gesture of cutting to signify that particular word—and yet, I was unable to cut any slack for other deaf people. *I* was doing my best; why wouldn't they? I was chronically judgmental about this. I felt that deaf people who signed instead of using their voices were letting the team down in some way; that they ought to pull themselves together and just *try*. Really, they should just get with the program. It was not until I renewed my connections with my childhood deaf friends and listened to their stories that I discovered that my occasional episodes of self-consciousness about my speech were amplified a hundredfold for them, stretching into unrelenting spasms of hurt in the face of other people's mockery of their skating, sliding, hiccoughing, ricocheting voices—sounds that hearing people horrifyingly describe as animal-like grunting; how do you think that makes deaf people feel?—and shunting them off into the shelter of the signing deaf community.

I had occasionally experienced renegade feelings of wistfulness about elements of deaf culture. I could see the beauty of sign's ballet, of the lean and pull of the body in the conversation's sway, and when I saw the deaf activist and actor Marlee Matlin in the movie based on Mike Medoff's play *Children of a Lesser God*, I saw how her signing was sensual and seductive. William Hurt fell in love with her.

I was in a place, now, where the use of hands for language was not only a practical skill for deaf people but also a desirable talent to enjoy, even when you didn't have to know it; even when you could hear and you could speak. In that classroom, the ability to sign was no indicator of whether you were deaf or hearing. In a way, the Auslan classroom was a modern-day version of Martha's Vineyard as described by Nora Ellen Groce in her 1985 book *Everyone Here Spoke Sign Language*. This was the community in Massachusetts where the high incidence of hereditary deafness created a culture in which not only were the hearing people bilingual in English and the Island sign language, but a hearing woman could say in reply to a question about those who were handicapped by deafness, "Oh, [. . .] those people weren't handicapped. They were just deaf." Up in front of the class-room, Jennifer signed with authority. With dignity. Always with humor. She smiled a lot. She wanted us not just to learn Auslan, but to *love* Auslan, the sweep and stretch and flow of it all. "Wriggle your fingers. Clench your fists. Relax your hands," she commanded us. "Stretch your eyebrows up high," she cried out. "Now frown, frown, frown," she urged us. But we couldn't frown. We crumpled into giggles instead. She laughed at us. "Frown!"

At the end of the term, Jennifer invited me to a party at her home where I met up again with some of my childhood friends from the deaf school: Carmel, Wayne, Dianne, Kay, and Kenneth. We exclaimed over each other, "How long has it been!" The party was a festive occasion. It was noisy in the way that all successful parties are, and everyone chatted happily with each other—some in signed English, some in spoken English, and occasionally some of us used a mix of mime and gestures when our fluency in either sign or spoken word was missing. We drank and ate through the afternoon, swapping our news and telling our plans.

When I talked with Kenneth about my "deaf project," he grew serious, dropping his lightness of spirit. He gripped me by my upper arms and said, "You must write about us. Tell our stories. People don't know about us, how hard we worked as children to learn to talk, to fit in. They think all deaf people sign. You know about the Stolen Generations, the Aboriginal Australian children taken away from their families by white bureaucrats? Well, we are the Forgotten Generation. We're the oral deaf kids no one wants to talk about. We've done well, but no one knows about us."

My stomach contracted with tension. I nodded. I gave him my promise. "Yes, I'll do that. I'll write about us."

I drove home from that party with the palms of my hands perspiring on the steering wheel. Kenneth's words played over and over, like tinnitus. I couldn't stop their noise in my brain.

Later I stopped by my mother's home and sat at her kitchen table. Nursing a cup of tea, I told her what Kenneth had said. I thought she might try to pacify me. I thought she might say something like, "Oh don't worry about what Kenneth said." But she didn't say that. She didn't try to pacify me. She went quiet for several moments and then said, her voice thick with the same worry I was trying to shake myself free of, "That's a big responsibility for you to shoulder. But you're up to it. You can do it."

6

A Six-Month Plan

I was exuberant. Everything was going well, and I was mindful of my good fortune. I had moved into my new apartment away from the inner city area but still close to the river, had enough paid work to keep financially afloat, and was buoyed by my friends' enthusiasm for my "deaf project." At the bottom of my red tote bag was a mess of notes on deafness scribbled on the torn-off edges of newspapers, lipstick-stained serviettes, yellow Post-its, and business cards. These were the accretions of the many conversations in coffee shops, conference rooms, and the verandahs of my friends' homes that I had had in between my policy projects for the Queensland Law Reform Commission and the Office of the Public Advocate. I went to conferences and seminars on deaf identity, deaf advocacy, and deaf education, and learned about advances in the diagnosis of deafness and hearing loss in newborn babies, along with the latest in cochlear implants and hearing technology. I shook off the weirdness of deaf people being *studied*—it was so anthropological, so Margaret Mead-ish—and stumbled into debates about signing versus speaking. One English hearing academic told me that he preferred to sign rather than speak. I thought this was peculiar at the time, and still do.

I felt as though I had come out of a closet. Everyone I met wanted to know about my "deaf project." How was I getting along with it? What was I learning? One friend was forthright in her excitement. "Great! Now you are letting us talk about it! I've been too scared to ask you questions before. You've always put up such a shield." I pressed her. "What do you mean?" She answered by telling her own story of discovery. She was a teenager when, through a casual comment to her father—"Don't I look Jewish in these photos?"—she stumbled on the realization that her mother was Jewish. More than this, almost all of her mother's family had died in concentration camps during World War II; her mother, then just a young girl of fourteen, had escaped from Germany on the eve of war. My friend's parents had kept this a secret from their daughters because her mother dreaded the consequences of exposure, even in the benign Brisbane suburbs of the 1970s, and her father supported her mother throughout her fear-locked silence. My friend said: "It's a strange thing to discover an identity you own that you didn't know about." Later, she wrote,

> Looking back, I think my determination to claim my Jewishness is an equal and opposite reaction to the power of the denial of Jewishness in our home [. . .] what is hidden and repressed in our natures will try to force its way into the open. I also believe that I was rejecting the shame attached to our identity.

I speculated about the possible parallels between this friend's experiences and mine. My mother had been vigilant and successful in her determination to raise me as a full-fledged hearing person. In fact, her vigilance in keeping me apart from the deaf world had bordered on inflexible. What emotions lay there? And why had I been such a willing and complicit partner for so long? My friend's use of the word "shame" shook me. Surely, my mother wasn't ashamed of my deafness? Or was *I* the person carrying that shame? No, no, no; that couldn't be right. No, it *wasn't* right. But there was no arguing with the fact that, historically, deafness was deemed a terrible affliction.

For the first time in my life, I immersed myself in reading other people's accounts of deafness. Stories from the Deaf community did not speak for me, as the framing of deafness as a separate linguistic and cultural entity had not shaped my life. Nor was I drawn to the militancy of identity politics that used terms such as "oppression" and "oppressors" to deride the ambitions of parents and educators to teach deaf children to speak. This seemed hostile and did not sit well with me; I had benefitted so much from integrating into the world of the maligned "oppressors." (Over time, as I became more attuned to the politics of Deaf rights, my views mellowed, but I still find the language of oppression unhelpful.)

As I cast around for stories of deafness and deaf people with which I could relate, I was troubled by how rarely I had met deaf characters in novels, despite being an avid lifelong reader. I had never read autobiographies by deaf writers, nor biographies of deaf people by either deaf or hearing writers. I wondered whether written stories of deafness—memoirs and fiction—shaped public perceptions or whether they simply responded to existing public perceptions of deafness. My question bubbled to the surface when I visited the Melbourne office of a national deaf children's organization.

There, I met with a public relations manager who showed me her office with housewifely pride. The walls were papered with newspaper from ceiling to desktop. Three walls of tiny black newsprint relieved only by the glare of a window pressed in on me. I leant across one of the desks to peer at the newsprint and saw that they were newspaper and magazine articles, many of which were illustrated with photographs of smiling children with hearing aids or cochlear implants. They told stories of how whole these young children were despite their deafness. Children were quoted as saying, "I can do anything even though I'm deaf" and "Just because I'm deaf, that doesn't mean I can't [insert activity]." It was creepy. It was like a scene from a Lenten appeal campaign from the 1950s exhorting Catholics to make donations to "save the pagan children." The only thing missing from the office was choral music, perhaps Handel's *Messiah*.

My discomfort about this evangelicalism, which struck me as enthusiasm gone mad, is at odds with my awareness that deafness and hearing loss shape the course of people's lives. I know that public awareness campaigns about services for deaf people, along with stories of hope and optimism, are important. Still, my discomfort persists.

I trawled up and down the book stacks in the university library, reading the spines of books by audiologists, special educators, speech pathologists, and other health professionals. The books seemed faded with age rather than with wear and tear; they had the dusty feel of books that were rarely picked up. And why would they be? With their cheerless titles, who would want to read them? The publishers' blurbs and abstracts revealed a tendency by most "expert" writers to portray deafness as a melancholy condition, or as a subject of caricature, or as a problem to be understood, overcome, or resolved. If these are the only books available to parents of deaf children, it is no wonder they are anxious and afraid for their deaf children's futures. The language used in so many titles of books, essays, videos, and other documents on deafness emphasized an "otherness" experienced by deaf people that is apparently bleak, hopeless, and lonely. Certain words and phrases were relentlessly reprised: "the isolated deaf child"; "from silence to speech"; "they grow in silence"; "broken silence"; "fitting into a silent world"; "her soundless world." They conjured up images of isolation, alienation, muteness, and a world of separateness "endured" by people with hearing loss. The crudeness of some of this "expert" writing was galling. The hearing writers wrote as if their words would never be read by deaf people, or as if the deaf reader—being so "alien"—could not possibly feel distressed or angered by the hearing writers' special claims of insights into the world of deafness. After just a few visits to the library, I wanted to push all these books off the shelves, sweeping them out of reach—and not just my reach, but everyone's reach. Medical and educational writing had a particularly apocalyptic tone about the consequences of deafness and the failure to deal with them. Go down this surgical pathway or use that technological intervention; put your child in a specialist or mainstreaming or inclusive classroom setting; tick the correct box, or all will be lost.

I switched to memoirs, hoping to find more sympathetic companions for my ruminations on the meaning of deafness in my life, but my early selections dismayed me. Helen Keller's *The Story of My Life* set the bar for saintliness and forbearance too high. Henry Kisor's dauntless cheerfulness in *What's That Pig Outdoors?* daunted me. David Wright was at war with his deafness: it was something to be overcome, resisted, avoided, healed, and even vanquished.

A friend had recommended Wright's 1969 memoir, *Deafness,* a slim volume with large print. I had weighed the book in my left hand as I contemplated it. Its pages were roughly cut at the edges rather than cleanly sliced. I liked this touch; the roughness gave the book the feel of a personal journal. It looked as though it had been written in privacy for an audience of only one or two intimate friends. I turned to the first page with some apprehension. I wanted to enjoy reading this memoir because the friend who recommended it to me had enjoyed it. But from the first few pages, I was filled with dread: this was not a man happy with his deafness. He found it a torment. I was shocked by his claim, "When I went up to Oxford, I resorted to private magic. I dropped the Christian name 'John' by which I was known at school and by my family. It was a symbolic exorcism of my deaf persona." He did not expand on this revelation, stating his case with just that single, short, sharp sentence. Wright's savagery toward himself and to his deafness repelled me. He regarded his deafness as such an awful, even evil, thing that he wanted it expunged from the record of his body and his soul. His hatred of his deafness agitated me. What else did he write in his memoir? I did not stay with his story to find out. He was not a person I wanted to spend time with. I trembled with anger. I wanted to find this man and confront him. Despite my long-held silence about my deafness, I had never repudiated it. I will never reject it.

I then embarked on a course of procrastination, slowing down my reading, because I felt bruised by these stories that set up deafness as the enemy within. I was particularly reluctant to read memoirs by hearing children of deaf parents such as Lennard Davis's memoir, *My Sense of Silence: Memoirs of a Childhood with Deafness,* and by hearing parents of deaf children such as *Deaf Like Me,* Thomas Spradley's account of his life with his deaf daughter, Lynn. Even now, I remain confronted and drained by the raining blows of grief in family narratives. I ploughed on with other books and withstood the assaulting language by squeezing my feelings into a compact space deep within me.

The persistent implication by these writers that deafness is a trauma was jarring, because it was so alien to my own experiences. I didn't feel traumatized or stricken in any way by my deafness, but when I stumbled across the title *The Deaf Child and His Family*, a fierce current whooshed through me, prompting me to e-mail a friend, "It strikes me as sad and peculiar that I would have been a source of such grief, panic, and anguish in my own family about something that holds no such feelings for me." My friend wrote back, "The grief for the child 'lost' or missing is a real experience and I am sure that your parents had some difficult times. Still they survived!" His flinty message was disheartening. It echoed what was in the literature: to be the parents of a deaf child was to believe that your child's future would be bleak, lonely, isolated; that your deaf child would endure a life of *otherness*, something alien to the life that you knew and that you had dreamt for all your children.

I had seen this fear as a child, not in my mother, but in a black-and-white movie on television one night about Helen Keller, the deaf and blind American scholar who was lauded during the mid-twentieth century as the world's most famous handicapped person. I would have been twelve years old—fully immersed in my hearing-world school life at All Hallows and long separated from my friends at the Gladstone Road Deaf School—when I first saw the movie *The Miracle Worker*. This was based on William Gibson's play, with the actor Anne Bancroft as the twenty-year-old teacher, Annie Sullivan, and Patty Duke as the child, Helen. I sat in a cane chair close to the glare of the television set, plugged into it by the cord of my stereo headphones. Our pet British bulldog, Cleo, with rheumy eyes and wheezing bellows of a chest, lay between me and the television set.

The movie opened with a scene of Helen Keller's mother screaming, "She can't see! She can't hear!" as she backed away from a baby's cot in a spookily dark room of night-shadows. It was awful. I was filled with her skin-shredding terror. The rest of the movie was taken up with people crying and shouting a lot over this wild child, Helen, struck blind and deaf through illness. I was appalled by it all—too young to sort out the theatrics of movie-acting from the emotional truth of the Helen Keller story—and did not dare ask myself, let alone my parents, if anyone had cried over me just because I was deaf. It would have been unthinkable for me to talk about it with either my sister or my brother, or with my school friends. I simply didn't have the emotional grammar for such an intimate conversation; I didn't even know that it was possible to talk about these things. Weren't you were supposed to absorb your worries and just roll along somehow? Which is what I did, distracted by the other preoccupations that shaped my life—keeping up with my school work, making friends, and holding on tight during the family storms that marked my father's pull away from the addictions of alcohol to the fellowship of Alcoholics Anonymous.

The memory of Helen Keller's weeping mother came back to me now, over and over again. I couldn't shake it off. I even went to the State Library to watch the film again; perhaps I'd imagined that terror? Perhaps if I saw the film again, I could erase that childhood memory and replace it with a different one? No. It was every bit as distressing as I had remembered.

I saw new things in it; saw the brutality of Annie Sullivan's teaching methods; the sentimentality of the scene where Helen Keller puts her hand under the tap with running water, and pronounces "wa-wa" as she finally understands the experience of naming what she sees and experiences. Saw too the fierceness of a mother's love, rejecting thoughts of defeat and other people's pessimism and pleas to be realistic, face facts. My throat constricted with the tension of holding back my tears; I was in a public place. I cried later, in the privacy of my home. I couldn't have told you then why I cried, there were so many reasons. I cried with the reawakened pain of my own parents' distress on discovering my deafness so many years ago; I cried for all those parents today who still endure that heartache on discovering their child is deaf. I cried, too, with frustration because all these tears were over something—deafness—that does not warrant such grief. To be deaf is not a death sentence. To be deaf means a different life; of course it does, but this does not mean it's a lesser life or a terrible life. And if it does, it shouldn't. Not today.

Finally, I lit on the idea of reading contemporary novels about deafness and deaf lives. There were not many, but Vikram Seth's *An Equal Music*, Frances Itani's *Deafening*, and T. Coraghessan Boyle's *Talk Talk* held me captive. None of these novelists were deaf, but they were able to imagine their way, with reasonable credibility, into deaf experiences. Curiously, however, all their deaf heroines have romantic relationships with hearing men; in the real world, most deaf women partner with deaf men. Despite the novels' being published within a few years of one another, they differ in their competing perspectives of deafness, which are shaped by the authors' thematic concerns—music, history, and identity. Together, they position the reader to respectively witness, be immersed in, and navigate experiences of deafness.

The novels reenergized me to seek out the memoirs of other contemporary deaf writers, such as Frances Warfield's journalistic memoir *Keep Listening*, Bainy Cyrus's plainspoken essay *All Eyes*, and Hannah Merker's meditations on her hearing loss, *Listening*. The women's writing resonated with the honesty and grittiness one might expect to see in private journals. While they evidently wrote for a reader other than themselves, their writing engaged with the task of reflection rather than persuasion—the paradox being that their memoirs thus *do* become persuasive accounts of deaf lives in all their possibilities. Warfield whips up the mayhem of a busy urban life with its jangle of noise and confusion; Cyrus exposes the shifts and strains in her relationships as a result of her deafness; and Merker sets herself a different quest, distilling her story to the rhythms of sounds.

These novelists and memoirists provided insights I did not even know I had been looking for. I will show how later, but now I can offer this: While sorrow was a pulse throughout most stories of deafness, those same stories told me other things. For a long time, I had been distracted by the apparently unhealthy and maddening preoccupation of so many writers with the themes of loneliness, alienation, grief, and the like. But historical and contemporary stories of deafness and memoirs of deaf people's lives also say a lot about the social, cultural, and educational values of the day; I saw how the individual fictional deaf characters and the deaf memoirists were pitted against the general swirl of life around them. So, even when I thought some of the stories were wrong, quarrelsome, exaggerated, or just plain silly, they all gave me fresh ways of understanding "deafness," "being deaf," and the lives of other deaf people.

It's an odd thing, but whenever I tried to justify my belief to my friends and companions over the unfolding months that deafness was not a terrible thing, I met with resistance. A few insisted on seeing my entire life as a sustained act of heroism in which I have triumphed over my "adversity" of deafness. Some suggested my frustration was really another expression of grief over my "hearing loss" (even when I explained with drawn-breath-impatience that I had not actually lost or mislaid my hearing; I never had it in the first place and so how could I experience it as a loss?). Others claimed I was in some sort of denial. They volunteered their unsolicited views; their list of claims was extensive. I countered their questions with my own questions and assertions:

"Surely, you've suffered because you haven't had a normal life?"— "What's normal?"

"Haven't people been cruel to you, called you names?"—"Most people are kind rather than cruel. Why do you want to think so badly of people?"

"What about music? What about all that you are missing out on there?"—"But I enjoy music! It mightn't be what you hear but *I* like it!"

My answers did not cut much ice. The husband of one friend was smug with his certainty: "You're wrong. That's not how you feel. You're just not facing up to things." Unbelievable. How dare he assume that *he* knew better than me the meaning of my deaf experiences? I wanted to hit him, and in fact, I did whack him across the shoulder. "You're not listening to me!" I shouted. I didn't care that people in the wine bar were staring at me, wondering at my anger. He infuriated me even more by nodding sanguinely, recrossing his gangly legs at his knees. He simply refused to be moved by the force of my emotions. My closest of friends—those who had been with me through my school and university years, and who had shared an office with me during my public service career—listened without skepticism to what I was saying. Two or three expressed a smiling surprise at my assertion of my deaf-self; "I've never thought of you as deaf," and "You've always just been, well, you!" I was, in turn, surprised by their surprise.

I attached more significance to my deafness than my friends did. I was uncertain whether to be troubled by this or whether to accept their comments as being made in the spirit of maintaining harmony. In the ensuing months, I flip-flopped from one view to the other. Writing this memoir guided me toward a conclusion of sorts. My deafness mattered to me, and I wanted this to be understood by my friends.

In my impatience to challenge people's perceptions of deafness and deaf people's lives, I accepted invitations to speak at meetings of parents with deaf children. One day I invited my mother along to a meeting. I had the idea that the young parents would enjoy listening to *her* stories rather than mine, especially since she was an older mother who could now talk with the perspective of time on her side. I was right; they did. One of the mothers wrote to me afterward: "Your mum really encouraged our parents with her wisdom and thoughts about the importance of family. Please thank her on our behalf for being so brave."

My mother had been doubtful but willing. She stood at the front of the room, her vulnerability under control, in all her formal dignity as if before a Senate Committee, and answered the young parents' questions precisely and without embellishment. Although she allowed herself the occasional flourish of humor, her answers leant toward accuracy rather than theater.

"Yes, the older children were very good. They were very keen to be helpful."

"No, they had never said anything resentful, nothing at all. If anything, they were defensive on Donna's behalf. They looked out for her."

"Yes, I taught Donna to read. I got into trouble from one of her teachers! But I believed in the importance of reading. She had to read. It was essential."

"No, I didn't want Donna to sign. I wanted her to speak. I wanted her to be able to play with the other children in our street. That's why we lived on the north side of the river, away from the deaf community."

"Well, there was a small group of us mothers. We got together and encouraged each other. We worked hard too, raising funds and even set up a secondhand clothes shop."

"A plan? Yes, I had a six-month plan. People would ask me, 'Are the six months up yet?' and I would answer, 'Just another six months to go!' and after five years, the six months were finally up. I felt ready to send her to All Hallows." This was a gamble for my parents in 1962. Transferring me from a special school for deaf children to a private girls school was a profound declaration of their hopes for me.

My mother's story of nuggetty determination emerged strongly, and I enjoyed hearing it again myself. She had never volunteered much to me, as I was growing up, about what it was like to be the mother of a deaf child during the 1950s, to be part of that pioneering group of mothers and fathers who placed their children in an oral education program intended to teach deaf children to speak their words out loud rather than to sign them silently but so expressively with their hands. She did not give herself the luxury of reflection. She was not of the generation that constantly weighs, measures, and examines the soul's register for debts and credits. She certainly did not use the word "grief" with me.

Instead, her language of grief had always been determinedly driven toward action, achieving and "righting" things. She preferred to talk of the incidents that made her laugh. She especially liked to talk about her role—along with some other mothers, Mrs. Perry, Mrs. Oakden, and Mrs. Nicholson—in establishing a secondhand clothes shop in Duncan Street, Fortitude Valley, to raise funds for the oral deaf preschool. A favorite anecdote was about one of the mothers, Tess Kinnane, who had kicked off her too-tight shoes one day. Throughout this particular day, the shop had filled with women bustling in and out of the change rooms, tossing tried-on items of clothing onto the floor, and rummaging for items from other boxes. The volunteer helpers had been frantic in their efforts to shepherd the discarded clothes back to the right places. Tess called out, "Hey, I've lost my shoes!" "What color were they, Tess?" One of the women clapped a hand over her mouth. "Oh dear, I sold them." Over the years, my mother repeated this story to me several times, and yet, each time she laughed as if for the first time and shook her head at the folly of it all.

When I asked my mother about her sorrow, she denied being terribly sad on finally having her suspicions about my deafness confirmed; well, perhaps just a little sad. She said, "My main feeling was one of relief. 'Oh, now I know! And I can do something about it!'" And "do something," she did. She saw she had a job to do, and like the country-born woman from central New South Wales that she was, she got on with it. I asked my mother who had been the source of her inspiration—had it been another family member? someone well-known? perhaps Helen Keller as a result of her visit to Australia just a few years before I was diagnosed as deaf? She shook her head and remained silent with her head bowed for several moments. She seemed to be struggling to compose herself. She looked back up at me and said, "No. I remember the day when I felt really fired up for you. I was visiting the Gladstone Road Deaf School and I saw this girl with red hair. Her name was Sandra. Oh, she was so bright! Clever as! Her face was just alive with intelligence. She had quick eyes and she was keen to learn. She wanted to learn everything." My mother smiled flickeringly at the memory. "And I thought to myself, if that girl Sandra can do it, then so will my daughter."

As we walked out of the parents' meeting toward the car park, my mother wiped her eyes with her floral-print handkerchief but spoke in her matter-of-fact voice. "They really shouldn't take it all so seriously," she said. She sounded irritated. "They are so *intense*." The thirty-five-minute drive back to her home was quiet. I concentrated on watching the traffic; my mother concentrated on her own thoughts. As I pulled up in front of her home, wondering what to say to break our silence, she turned swiftly to me and said, "Thank you, love," in a tone that allowed for no idle last-minute chit-chat. But, in the instant that she put her feet down outside the car to stand on the footpath, she leaned around, turned back to me, and in a voice clouded with wonder and sadness and history and loss and all those other emotions that fill our hearts in the early hours of dawn when we are trying to muster our hopes to go on, she said, "You know, Tess Kinnane and I were just like those parents today, when we were at Yeronga with you and Sharon," and closed the car door before I could reply. In her voice and in her words, I heard an admission of her own long-ago fears and understood that courage is pragmatism in motion. In the turmoil of the uncertain moment, you don't feel brave. As the waves of heartache, fear, and distress wash over you, what you do is this one thing. You let yourself give in to the tidal pull of doing what must be done.

In the midst of all this activity, Damian came into my life. It was summer, a time of Sunday barbecues and drinks on friends' balconies in the evenings. He was a friend of a friend. I had encountered him around the edges of my social circle before but had not paid him any attention despite his lively personality and an infectious laugh that made everyone smile. Everyone, that is, except his wife. Her chilly presence had acted as a deterrent to even the most innocent of small talk between us. But at one of these social gatherings, it was apparent that his wife was no longer his wife, and so it came about that Damian handed me a glass of wine and said, "You've got a hearing problem." He inflected his voice to turn it into a question. The other party guests jostled around us, opening bottles of beer and uncorking wine. Some fuss was being made about the choice of music to be played.

I gave my usual answer. "No, I don't have a hearing problem, I'm deaf," and as usual, my answer created a ripple effect. Startled. Nonplussed. Not sure what to say next. I was obdurate; that didn't help. I took another sip from the glass of wine and looked around the room at the others. It dawned on me that the thumping sensations in my ears were the marching reverberations of Carl Orff's *Carmina Burana* coming out of the stereo system. I felt Damian's gaze on me. I looked up at him—he was unusually tall but did not have that slouching habit of some tall men—and I wondered why I had not noticed before how his honey-colored hair was always tousled as if he had just emerged from the surf. I glanced away from him but my eyes strayed back toward his eyes; they were dark green, just like the ocean on an overcast day. He looked thoughtfully back at me, and then it was his turn to catch me off-guard. "I'm interested. Would you mind talking with me about it?" In Damian's refusal to be rattled by me, I saw sincerity, and so I relented.

That conversation led to an exchange of e-mails that led to a dinner invitation, and before long we found ourselves settling into a shaky rhythm of movies, dinners, coffee breaks, text messages, and phone calls. Sometimes we went out by ourselves; occasionally we met up with other friends and family. We were both busy; our lives felt hectic; our families, friends, and work all conspired to keep our diaries full. It was the usual routine of courtship—we talked, laughed, amazed each other—but I did not feel casual or routine about my feelings. Damian asked me a lot of questions about my deafness. He wanted to read what I had written about it. He talked as though he was trying to understand all the elements that made me "tick." I was bemused by this, but also flattered; his curiosity about me was seductive. His enthusiasm for me combined with his gentle nature seemed to establish him as someone I could rely upon. Even his height seemed a persuasive credential. I pressed my joy close to myself; so closely, that I didn't tell anyone about my bursting hopes that, just possibly, love had come into my life when I was least expecting it.

7

Music Lessons

Damian e-mailed me regularly between our excursions to the movies, dinners, and coffee outings. He would also telephone me from his work for a quick chat or send me text messages on my mobile phone. I looked forward to logging into my in-box and seeing his name in bold type, right there in the midst of all my work e-mails. Damian. I always clicked onto his name first, ahead of the other e-mails, to read his latest bit of news. When my mobile phone buzzed with the chirrup of an incoming text message, I would rummage urgently through my bag or around the top of my desk to find it, hoping that the chirrup signaled yet another message from him. In this way, even though we did not see each other all that often, I felt a bond of intimacy building between us. I liked to think about him; and I liked to think that each telephone call, e-mail, and text message from him meant that he was thinking of me too. Late one evening, he sent me an e-mail about the French film festival. Would I like to go? Yes! I was free most nights! I waited to hear back from him.

Growing up deaf in a hearing family draws on the same skills needed for walking across one of those wobbling rope-and-plank bridges cast up high across rain forest creeks: both demand agility in moving back and forth across borders, balance in mind as well as body, and confidence tempered by caution. The difference between the two tasks is that the first one continues lifelong, and the second is a one-off journey completed in a matter of minutes, tension-filled though they might be.

As a child, I sat through mealtimes at the dinner table—that place and time in the early evening when we gathered as a family—in a daze of incomprehension. I had the choice of eating what was on the dinner plate before me while forgoing watching what was being said around the table, or I could watch the words being mouthed by my parents, sister, and brother, and let the sausages and vegetables on my plate cool. I understood what was being said only if I made the concentrated effort to do so—forking in a mouthful of mashed potato in between glances at the words sailing across the table—or if I insisted on their repeating what they had just said in the moments that I had my eyes down to the plate. I would pull at my mother's arm and assert myself: "What are you saying?" When a friend asked me to give an example of the sorts of conversations I might have missed out on during those childhood mealtimes, I scoffed at him. "If I knew the answer to that question, I wouldn't have missed out, would I?"

But in hindsight, I understand now why I do not share my family's casual knowledge about this relative and that neighbor: the incidents, tragedies, and joys that peppered their lives must have been the grist for those dinnertime conversations. I never did catch up; I still have many gaps in my stocktaking of who did what with whom and when. This makes me feel foolish. Every cry of "You *must* remember that/her/him!" feels like an accusation, as if I have been remiss in some way. I made my way through a world, at home and outside, in which people's mouths opened and closed in a rhythm that did not always make sense to me. When they did not face me and speak directly to me, I was tense with wondering: what had they said? could I ask? or was I asking too much, too often? I was never fully in the know and lived with the chronic discomfort of cluelessness: what's going on? It was as if the actions around me were taking place on a film that had torn away from its spool on the projector, and was now flapping around and around, casting confusing shadows and images against the wall. At home, I dealt with this by submerging myself in my own imaginative world and letting the voices of my family slurry above me and around me. It was simply a sludge of sound, the rise and fall of volume and pitch. I would search my family's faces and see what meaning I could read into their expressions. I don't recall any sense of exclusion. Not really.

After all, our family life was held together loosely by the conventions of the time. If she was not at work, my mother could usually be found either in the kitchen preparing our next meal, in the piano room ironing our clothes, or downstairs watering the yard; occasionally, she might walk down the road to have a cup of tea and slice of cake with Enid, her good friend. My father always seemed to be "out"; he was not a strong presence in the house, a common enough condition for fathers during the fifties and sixties. I was content to play with my dolls (measuring up and sewing new clothes for them) or read my library books or, as I got older, do my homework, while my sister talked on the telephone in the lounge room and my brother strummed his guitar and sang in his bedroom. Sometimes, I felt miffed about not understanding everything that was going on or being said. Mostly, I remember the calmness of being left alone, although I did experience occasional shivers of paranoia, especially if my insistence on having something repeated to me was met with an impatient "Oh, it doesn't matter." I would wonder: "Are they talking about me? Have I done something wrong?"

All those fractures in my conversations around the dinner table with my family, in the classroom with my teachers, and on the playground with my classmates, and with my work colleagues and friends over the ensuing years lay beneath my skin. This is why, when Damian did not follow up his e-mail invitation to me about the French film festival, the discomfort of broken communication was familiar to me. I didn't panic, not immediately, but I did sink slowly beneath the rising tide of worry. What had I done wrong? What cues had I missed? Had Damian said something to which I had not reacted properly? To distract myself, I did what I always did: I turned to my work, I had much to do. Just as I had pressed my joy to myself, so I kept quiet about my fears.

When I was a little girl with wispy hair tied in two bunches, I wanted to write books. One afternoon, I gathered together some sheets of paper, packed them into a neat block on the top of my chenille-covered bed, knelt by the edge of the bed, gripped my HB pencil in my right hand, and gouged out a title: *My Stories*. But I could go no further. Despite the urge to transpose into writing those sounds that I was learning to read, I could not translate the pictures I saw on my mind's screen into word images on the page before me. I had no voice within me that would let me put my stories down on paper. I felt trapped inside a balloon, straining to break through its membrane.

In the dragging days of Damian's silence, I felt myself drawn back to the oppression of that balloon. I did not know what to say or how to say it.

He broke the silence. Finally. But the words he chose to end his e-mail of apology quickened my breath. "Sometimes, silence is golden."

"Oh no!" Damian grabbed his head with both hands and bent double at the waist. "I wasn't even thinking of you being deaf. I wasn't, you know, I didn't mean . . ." By now, he was jigging his knees up and down in a hyperactivity of remorse. We were sitting on my balcony overlooking the courtyard garden made green and leafy during the drought by regular dousings of grey water caught in laundry buckets. I shifted my seat to be in the shade; it was a bright sunny morning with the first bite of autumnal coolness. Damian had brought baked bagels still warm from the oven, and I had made a pot of English Breakfast tea. I teased him. "For such a Mr. Havachat, why on earth would you write such a thing?" My question stilled his movements. He looked up from his mea culpa position, saw that my curiosity was genuine, and said with the hesitancy that comes with not wanting to make the other person feel foolish, "Brian Poole and the Tremeloes?" He sang a few bars, tapping his right foot in time to the beat. I shook my head. I had never heard of either the band or their 1967 hit song. I was eleven years old when "Silence Is Golden" hit number one in the United Kingdom; their fame had bypassed me, and I still lagged behind in my music history forty years later. I had missed a whole generation of rock 'n' roll because I could not pick out the words of the lyrics through the mesh of the instruments.

I did not tell Damian this but I could see from the uncertain expression on his face that he thought my world of music must be limited. I chose to ignore what I saw; it was easy to do. I was practiced at it. Anyway, it was not the time to stand at my deaf lectern; it was the time for laughing and for consoling and for telling each other our news. We hugged our good-byes that morning, and I tasted the promise of seeing each other again on our lips.

This incident, small though it was, made me stop and think about the place of music in my life. The words "music" and "deafness" do not usually make happy bedmates in the minds of most hearing people. My own weak musical literacy often creates a disruptive ripple in conversations, causing the other person either to breathe in sharply with disbelief or breathe out with a whoosh of dismay. Even though I grew up in a house of music as a child—there was always a record playing or a radio turned on or a guitar being strummed—I approached the act of listening to music as a task. It was a pleasurable task, but it was something to focus upon rather than to relax with. I didn't breathe in the music as it floated across the air; I *willed* it into myself.

My earliest recollection of music was watching my mother play on an old-fashioned pianola installed in the front lounge room of our home. I would have been three or four years old, and I alternated between watching the rotation of the paper reel with its Braille-like music notations or lying on the floor to watch the pedals as my mother pumped them with her feet. I cannot remember hearing the music itself, but I must have felt its thump and fall through the pianola's heavy timber frame, perhaps in the same way that Helen Keller described in an essay, "The Finer Vibrations." She wrote that when she kept her hand on the piano case, she could feel the strum of melodies, but could not easily distinguish a tune that was sung.

My mother encouraged my interest in music even when she must have been uncertain about how much of it I was able to take in. She bought a miniature piano-organ for me when I was six years old. A luscious honey-gold color, it was the topic of the day for "Show and Tell" in Mrs.

Mason's class. A few years later, a full-sized piano was dragged into the dining room and my mother arranged for me to have piano lessons from Mrs. Pringle, who lived on the top of a hill a few streets away. The first year of my Friday afternoon lessons was spent on tunes such as "Row, Row, Row Your Boat" and "Polly Put the Kettle On." It was a step up from playing the metal triangle I had been issued in grade four at All Hallows. The transparency of this effort by the teachers to include me in the music classes had not escaped me, even then, even as a nine-year-old. I felt foolish, not just because I was saddled with a tinny instrument that I was told to strike every now and then—the other girls had "proper" instruments such as violins, recorders, flutes—but also because I felt I could not reasonably protest. My piano lessons included performing for the Australian Music Examinations Board. I look back now and marvel at the composure of the examiners and their kindness toward me. I encountered one examiner a few times; she was a high-profile pianist, but far from being intimidating, she always smiled at me with great warmth, as if urging me to succeed in my musical efforts. After several years of piano tuition, I was able to play a reasonably tuneful rendition of Beethoven's "Für Elise." (At the time, I did not know about Evelyn Glennie, the deaf concert percussionist from Scotland: a pity; I might have been inspired to do more.)

So, while I enjoyed listening to music, I usually discovered songs and musicians through conversational stumbles such as the one with Damian. They rarely came to me unbidden, because I did not have the habit of play-ing radio music as the accompaniment to my days and nights. When I was at school and at university, I could not join in conversations about the latest hit-parade songs. It was like watching a foreign-language movie without the subtitles: I saw and heard my friends' excitement in sharing what they knew, but I could not understand the details and did not like to ask. More than this, I was impressed by my friends' extensive knowledge of music and wondered how they found so much time to sit down and listen to so much radio. Of course, they didn't. While I crouched next to the honey-colored Astor radiogram in the lounge room and either pressed my hearing aid to one of the speakers or put on my headphones, they turned on their transistors and absorbed their music with the same unthinking skill as breathing. I was baffled once by the enthusiasm that a school friend, Janeane, showed for listening to carpenters; my bewilderment grew when she said that her boyfriend liked listening to them too. Why the delight in the rasp of saw, the knock of hammer? When my sister came home after work with a new LP record, "A Song for You," I felt an exploding "pop!" of understanding. The red cover was illustrated with a white heart beneath a black stylized inscription, "Carpenters." I studied that record in the same way that others study an area of esoteric knowledge; I wanted to keep up with my friends.

My not knowing contemporary music meant that I lacked an important currency for teenage conversation. It also meant that I missed the significance of certain world events. Back then, music was *the* vehicle for reflecting back to society the revolutions that were taking place—feminism (Helen Reddy's "I Am Woman"), sexual liberation, antiwar movements, Black Power, recreational drug taking, and more. Much of this wafted over my head: with the exception of the Vietnam War, I was oddly unmindful of the scale of historic social and political events taking place at the time. (But perhaps I was not so odd. Perhaps it is the nature of "history" to be invisible to us at the time of its making; we think of it as something that happens in the past.)

The sound of radio—be it the news, talk shows, classical music, the best of the sixties, or the latest in indie rock—adds to the texture of our daily lives: it does not just create a curtainlike backdrop to our activities; it drops a web of invisible sound threads crisscrossing suburbs, cities, and entire continents to connect one lone person to the next. I like this image of being connected to my neighbors and friends by such spidery sound threads, but in reality, I cannot stand the shirring of radio-rustle in the air around me. It is an irritant, intruding into whatever it is that I am attending to at the moment, whether it is a conversation, a book, or work. I enjoy music only if I sit down, put my headphones on, and listen to it in a deliberate act of concentration, and then I enjoy it immensely, letting the pulse of the music play not just through my hearing aids and into my ears, but also beat across the soft skin on my chest, seeping into the core of my bones. I especially like it if I have a copy of the lyrics so that I can give meaning to the sounds I can hear. A long time ago, in a rare act of collaboration, my father transcribed for me the words of the Rolf Harris song "Two Little Boys."

I also enjoy gifts of music. This detail hit me hard one Christmas, not long before my forty-fifth birthday, when a work colleague gave me a present. I was surprised by the gesture of the gift from my colleague, but when I unwrapped the paper from the small square and saw that it was a compact disc of songs by the Indigo Girls, I was momentarily bemused. In my adult life, no one had ever given me a gift of music. No record, no tape, no sheet music. Nothing. That compact disc was the first time I had been given anything musical since my childhood. I played it over and over again for months, as much for the joy of the gift itself as for the music.

Damian's song of silence came to life. The words came to pass. *Talking is cheap, people follow like sheep / Even though there is nowhere to go [. . .] / How many times will she fall for his line? / Should I tell her or should I keep cool . . .* Damian said he would call me, come to my home again the next weekend. He did not call me; he did not come to my home. The contagion of his silence settled like dust over my days, and my quest to better understand my deaf-self stalled. I attended to the more urgent task of rising above this latest disappointment.

8

But My Eyes Still See

In the following weeks, I thought often about that sunny morning with Damian on the balcony, and I remembered other things. Things that should have alerted me to the fragility of his feelings for me. I remembered the pulse of other emotions on Damian's face. I saw, in hindsight, more than his uncertainty about my relationship with music; I also saw his conflict about me. I had underestimated the urgency of his anxiety about continuing his relationship with me. He had much going on in his life. He said it was too much. It was impossible, he said. He was a single parent; he could not do justice to our relationship and honor his family obligations at the same time. "Duty before love," he said with a lilting effort at humor. I had argued mildly with him. "But Damian, we are only in the early days of getting to know each other. Can't we just roll along as we've been doing?" He had not answered my question. Instead, we found ourselves talking about our friends, our work, and our families. We had hugged our goodbyes, but as for tasting the promise of seeing each other? Perhaps I imagined this as I watched Damian walk backward down the stairs, his eyes on me all the way to the entrance of the apartment building. In my first disbelief at Damian's withdrawal from my life, the Tremeloes' song of mute distress felt like an epitaph.

.

My words here are orderly. The passage of time and the love of friends have allowed me to tidy up my thoughts and to put them down now on this page, steadily and at the rate of one word at a time. Still, I cannot describe the knifing pain that I experienced, along with the whimpering confusion, feverish anger, and hot resentment with life—and with a God whose reliability I was already dubious about—without resorting to the language of melodrama. But it seems that through no fault of either Damian's or mine, the collapse of our friendship triggered in me a collapse of confidence in my judgment, not just about love but about life. I had been so full of hope for the possibilities of our friendship, and now I was full of anger. How many more losses and how much more grief was I supposed to endure? Surely there was a quota posted somewhere and just as surely I was double-dipping and someone else was skipping out on their fair share of sorrow? It didn't help that I was lurching toward the twentieth anniversary of my son's death; I was in the midst of organizing a commemorative ceremony for Jack with my family at the local Catholic church, St. Agatha's. It also didn't help that so much of my reading about deafness was soaked in grief and trauma.

As I trawled obsessively over the details of my short friendship with Damian, I caught myself reassessing his every gesture, look, laugh, and conversational gambit. In that game of revising romantic history, so familiar to anyone who has had her heart broken, I drilled for clues and came up with new interpretations of our friendship and his abandonment. See, even now I continue to change my words to describe that event: loss, withdrawal, abandonment. Which was it? How did it really go? My doubts about my judgment spilled over into my investigation of my deaf life. After all, wasn't everyone—those writers of the trauma of deafness and those friends insistent on challenging my explanations—trying to tell me that my deafness was a loss and that I was denying it? Well, *was* I denying it? Had I been too glib? Were there other interpretations of my life that I was turning a blind eye to, casting in a Pollyanna-like glow? I wanted to be honest; it was important to be honest.

In my mind's eye, I kept seeing the tear-streaked faces of parents at those support meetings and conferences I attended. One mother, clutching a crumpled white tissue in her hand, had asked me in a voice filled with the effort to be composed, "Is there anything your mother could have done better or differently for you?" before she fell back onto a chair in a crumple of tears, more wet tissues, and stray hair across her forehead. I had been mesmerized by the depth of her sorrow, swelling as it did from fear and preemptive guilt. This mother was readying herself to plead guilty for all the actions and inactions she was yet to take on behalf of her young deaf son and daughter. Along with her assumption of guilt, she wanted pre-emptive absolution for the life that she feared for her deaf children; would they endure intolerably different lives from their hearing children, lives of inadequate education, menial jobs, isolation, and perhaps even exclusion from love? I owed her, and the other parents, my honesty. I had told her, "No, every decision my mother made on my behalf was the right one." My voice had been loud. I had been firm "There is nothing that she did that I would wish that she hadn't done." The mother looked unconvinced. I tried again. "Although I do very much wish that she had not cut my hair so short." The mother smiled wetly at this, along with the other parents in the room who joined together in a free-fall of laughing solidarity. I heard again, too, the voice of another mother who asked, "Who will love my daughter as much as I love her?" And of course, her question snagged on my own fear: which man would love me?

During this time, I went browsing in a music store at the local shopping center in search of sheet piano music by the choral group Secret Garden. I listened to their songs of contemplation when I meditated, and wanted to teach myself to play their songs on my small upright Samick piano. The sound system in the music store that Saturday belted out excerpts from swing, blues, jazz, rock, pop, disco, rap, and world music, but it only stocked fat songbooks with titles such as *Easy Classics for Children* and *The Best of the Sixties*. No single-song sheet music.

I turned to a plump woman in a wheelchair next to me and commented, "Isn't it a shame that you can only buy music in fat books?" She didn't acknowledge me, and I thought that I had perhaps offended her with my use of the word "fat," but when I kept looking at her, she gave a start and

said, "I'm sorry, I'm deaf, what did you say?" I giggled and said "So am I!"
I was gleeful at the two of us, both deaf, browsing through rows of sheet
music. I asked the other deaf woman what instrument she played. When
she answered, "I'm trying to learn the piano," her voice held that sound of
profound deafness, as if she was speaking through a membrane of water
blocking her throat, or perhaps as if she was trying to swallow a yawning
boredom. I wondered if I sounded like that; my vanity prickled; I hoped
not. The woman went on to explain that she was in a music group; everyone else in the group was hearing. I boggled a bit at this. My eyes widened. I remembered my school-days' envy of my classmates heading off to
orchestra practice, when I had been fascinated—was *still* fascinated—by
their skill in playing their own instruments while at the same time hearing, and staying in tune, in time, with so many other instruments around
them. "Oh my, that's brave of you. Are you any good? Can you play the
piano well?" She laughed un-selfconsciously. "I don't know!" I laughed too,
but uncertainly. She went on. "I don't mind. I just like learning. If I was
perfect at music or anything, I'd have nothing new to learn." I recounted
this conversation to my friends at the swimming pool the next morning,
whereupon we all laughed together. The other woman had finished her
explanation by saying, "Actually, I take out my hearing aids when I'm playing in the group so I'm not distracted by the noise of all the instruments."

I was in the mood for light music and books. It was time to shake off the
gloom that cloistered my days. I turned to Vikram Seth's novel *An Equal
Music*. I had read this novel several years earlier, and fallen in love with
Seth for writing a novel that so beautifully combined music, deafness, and
romantic love; with the deafened concert pianist, Julia, for being such a
gutsy, talented, and attractive heroine for whom hearing loss was *not* a
tragedy; and with the flawed hero, Michael, also a concert musician, for
loving her, deafness and all. The very act of reading *An Equal Music* had
filled me with mellow stirrings. It was time to reread it.

    In most stories that feature deafness and deaf people, the reader sees
or experiences the life of the deaf character through the perceptions and

experiences of the hearing narrator. And so it is in Vikram Seth's novel of love and music. I learnt what it meant for Julia to be deaf by observing Michael's grief-stricken reactions to her. I witnessed the "broken transmission" effects—like the worn needle of a record player skipping across an old long-play record—that occur in communication between a deaf person and a hearing person, especially if the deaf person has not disclosed her deafness. And I saw, too, the lengths that Michael went to, in his efforts to protect Julia upon discovering her deafness.

Seth wrote about music in detail, describing both the sensation of deafness for the hearing reader and the mysterious variousness of musical sound for deaf readers. His descriptions called up my own early memory of sound: as a child, I liked to stand under the shower and hear the noise of the water raining down onto my shower cap. I would tighten the cap down over my ears, like a helmet and, with my eyes closed, I would capture the water's roar in stereo. But one evening, I let myself be lost for too long in this reverie: the shower curtains whipped back; I opened my eyes; my mother's face, a twist of terror, filled the frame. Her fright fled on seeing me, standing there, wet and alive. She looked angry then, the anger that comes with the gut-wrenching relief of discovering that all is well with your child. I saw her snap, "What are you doing? I heard the noise, the water coming down on your head . . ." I was staggered. She could hear the noise of the shower from *outside*? This was surely impossible? Evidently not. From then on, I only let myself taste the sound of roar in small guilty doses by ducking my head in and out of the shower, alternating between the crash of water belting down on my plastic shower cap and the soft thrumming of waterfall on my neck and chest. The sounds were as different as pebbles and satin.

In this spirit of playing with sounds, I sat with my copy of *An Equal Music* tagged with yellow flags and heavily underlined throughout, slipped a CD into my Bose system, and tried to comprehend the music Vikram Seth wrote about: Haydn's Quartet in A major, op. 20, no.6; Mozart's Sonata for Piano and Violin in E minor, K. 304/300c; Bach's Contrapunctus 1 from *The Art of the Fugue*; Beethoven's String Quintet in C minor, op.

104; Schubert's Trout Quintet; Vivaldi's "Manchester" Sonata No. 1 in C major; and Vaughan Williams's "The Lark Ascending." It was a chastening experiment. No matter how hard I concentrated, those first musical sounds of violins and pianos playing in harmony always petered away to a tiresome crush of instruments from which no melodies found their way to me. I just didn't have the right hearing capacity, even with both my hearing aids turned up to full volume, to understand what I was listening to. This made me curious. What *did* hearing people hear? Seth described the act of playing of Beethoven's music as "the steeple-chase-cum-marathon, the ethereal, jokey, unpausing, miraculous, exhausting quartet in C sharp minor, which he composed a year before his death." I was incredulous; all I heard was a messy blur. But in another passage, Seth wrote of Michael, "I sit with my head in my hands, as Mozart drops note by note into my mind." This, I *did* understand; I too experienced some music as an entire body and spirit experience, not just an aural event. Like Michael, I absorbed music in my mind, not just my ears, letting it enter into my whole being.

I caught myself enjoying Seth's novel on two levels: first, I followed the revival of Michael and Julia's love affair; and second, I watched out for how Seth described Julia's hearing loss and the other characters' responses to her deafness. He disclosed Julia's hearing loss subtly, yielding up her secret to the reader bit by bit. When Julia and Michael met again for the first time after a separation of several years, Michael observed a change in Julia: "There is an intentness to her gaze." I understood this clue about Julia's deafness immediately, and also understood that Michael had *not* got it. Michael, perhaps like many hearing readers, interpreted this as a demonstration of Julia's intensity of emotion for him, that perhaps she still loved him after all these years apart. Seth repeated the image of "the attentive gaze" throughout his novel. I wondered about my gaze on Damian's face. How had *he* felt? Michael finally learnt that Julia was deaf when her young son, Luke, revealed it accidentally:

"I didn't get that. You're mumbling."

"It's the way I speak," says Luke with sudden sullenness.

"But you spoke so clearly just a little while ago."

"'That's because mom finds it hard to hear me. She's deaf . . . Oops!" he claps his hands over his mouth.

Luke's inadvertent revelation and his white-faced desperation to take back his words were tinged with horror, as was Michael's disbelief on learning of Julia's deafness.

Now, all this suspense, secrecy, revelation, horror, and anguish are well and good in fiction, and I was drawn into the drama of it all as an involved reader, but in real life, the harboring of secrets is the foundation stone for unnecessary grief. I was appalled on behalf of the little boy, Luke, by the drive for secrecy. What was so terrible or shameful or confronting about his mother's deafness? Seth used secrecy as a plot device because Julia was worried about the impact on her concert-playing career once her deafness became public knowledge. Okay; so let's accept that for a moment. This still does not explain Julia's withholding from Michael, the man she once loved and apparently continued to love; nor does it justify co-opting her son into the guilt that secrets confers. My own parents and siblings—indeed, my entire extended family of aunts, uncles, cousins, nieces, and nephews; I had no grandparents, they had died young—never showed the slightest inclination to compress my deafness into a wafer of secrecy. Far from it. They were open, chatty, and proprietary about my deafness. Elderly aunts and uncles would ooh and aah at Christmas parties, weddings, and funerals over my academic successes. "Imagine that," shaking their heads. "All that even though you're deaf," sighing. One cousin, Ian, having convinced himself as a teenager that the photo of a little girl on the charity collection tins on the tables in his local milk bar, *The Blue Bird Cafe*, was me, encouraged his mates to put their loose change into the tins. Other cousins would bail me up at family festivities or call me at home about this newspaper article or that radio show about deaf people. This happened a lot during the time of the militant deaf students' movement at the Gallaudet University, a liberal arts university for deaf students in the United States. My sister routinely rang me in a hurry of news-giving to tell me about yet another deaf person she had met, spoken with, heard about, seen in the distance at a shopping center, or who she had just learned attended the same church as me. It was the same with my parents' friends too; they were uniformly stout in their assessment, "Of course, your mother worked very hard on your behalf." They were all interested; they were all keen to be in the know, to be a part of my deaf life. Sharing stories of other deaf people and quizzing me about my deafness helped them forge their bond with me.

My sister's second son, Simon, was particularly interested, and as a seven-year-old boy, his curiosity took a forensic turn. His teacher had taken his class on an excursion to a sensory-education unit where children were placed in darkened rooms to experience blindness, sent into wobbling-walk tunnels to experience mobility difficulties, and wore headphones to learn about deafness. This was all supposed to teach the children empathy for others. Simon had boasted to his class teacher, "My auntie, well, she's deaf!" For several weeks after this excursion, he would gaze at my hearing aid, reach his hand up toward it, and ask, "Can I have a go?" To which I would take my hearing aid out of my ear, bend down and hold it to his ear, and watch his face crease into a grin of satisfaction as he listened to its whistling squeal. After some weeks of this, my sister observed that Simon's hearing appeared to be erratic. He didn't always answer her when he was called. Perhaps his hearing wasn't as sharp as it should be? That would explain his interest in my hearing aid, wouldn't it? Ever vigilant about the need for quick action, she booked him in for an audiology appointment. Her vigilance grew into alarm during the appointment; in the waiting room, she kept looking at her watch; the audiologist was certainly taking his time in there with young Simon; things must be *really* serious. At last, the audiologist came out of the test room. His face was full of good humor. Simon's pale face, on the other hand, was a study; it was filled with the intensity of doom that sparrow-boned seven-year-old boys can convey when they see their world collapse around them in a brick pile of broken hopes. The audiologist spoke first. "I take it that Simon's aunt is deaf?" My sister gasped, "Yes." "Well, it seems that our Simon here would like to be deaf too. He wants to wear a hearing aid like hers." The audiologist turned to Simon and clapped a hand on Simon's shoulder. "But you don't need one, do you?" Simon cast his eyes down and shook his head. "Oh, for

God's sake!" My sister unloosened her relief at the news and irritation at the wasted time; she laughed later, when she retold the story of Simon's efforts to be deaf. Twenty years later, the story's repeated telling had given it the sheen of family legend, the sort that gets retold every Christmas Day. "Remember the time when Simon told that guy he could hear the quiet sounds but not the loud ones!" More laughter.

Back in Seth's novel, *An Equal Music*, following Michael's discovery of her deafness, Julia wrote a letter to him in which she gave a vividly precise description of deafness as another sensation, "not soundlessness." She wrote that she felt as if she was "muffled in cottonwool" and "then suddenly things bang out at me." I understood Julia's sense of fragility, perhaps even of danger. She knew that sounds were "out there" that she was not aware of; her sense of personal safety was compromised. Michael's letter of reply to Julia was filled with his confusion, love, and more questions. His efforts to learn about deafness mimicked my real world efforts to understand hearing. He tried to tune in to the world of deafness by reading a book about it while listening to music, a recording of Schubert's string quintet: "It is to the sounds of that music that I make my first acquaintance with the elaborate chaos that lies behind the tiny drumskins of my outer ears." In this same scene, Michael wondered about his place in Julia's life now that she was deaf. In contemplating the role of music in their love for each other, he raised the specter of the role of sound in all its communicative power—and by implication, silence in all its desolation—in forging and sustaining the bonds of love between two people. I fretted briefly; was this the key to understanding what had happened between Damian and me?

Prior to meeting Damian, my romantic relationships had been largely silent about my deafness. Being deaf was such an elemental part of my "I-ness," that I did not pay much attention to it, either with care or grievance. In her drive to assert my normalcy (and possibly also because of her distaste for any scent of self-pity or crutch-seeking), my mother had deflected my early tentative efforts at talking about the implications of my deafness. Once, when I was twelve years old, I asked her whether my deafness would affect my boyfriend prospects. "No! Not at all!" she cried out. I was gratified. Momentarily. My mother went on, "You're a very kind girl and you sew well."

For whatever reason, I had never talked at any length about my deafness with the men in my life, all of whom were hearing. Not with my first boyfriends at university, nor with the man to whom I was married for a short time, nor later with Jack's father or the men I dated after him. I would have answered any questions about my deafness that they cared to ask, but they did not ask many, and I did not volunteer much; they must have tried to second-guess my needs. In hindsight, I suspect that they simply understood my deafness as an auditory loss rather than as something that might shape my sense of self. Admittedly, Seumas had been openly curious, but his curiosity circled around the mechanics of deafness, hearing, and language. At times this would take a theatrical turn; he liked to mouth words at me to test whether I could understand him, and when I replied in full voice, he would fall about in a wheezing heap of joy. His questions seemed to have little to do with getting to know me; they were not designed to improve his understanding, or mine, for that matter, of what my deafness might mean for our friendship. I did not take his curiosity seriously, or reflect upon his questions beyond the conversations in which they took place.

In my romances, my brief marriage, and my relationship with Jack's father, we did not ignore my deafness entirely. That would have been silly, but any references to my deafness revolved around domestic matters such as having a telephone with a volume control adapter, or checking the seating and lighting arrangements when we went out to restaurants or to the movies, or arranging for a friend to help me look after Jack when his father was away from home on work business. (When Jack was born, I felt a secret twinge of betrayal when I expressed my relief that he was not deaf. I didn't know who I was betraying, but the emotion was there all the same.) It wasn't that I deliberately censored our conversations to strip them bare of deafness. No, it was more that my deafness did not spring to mind as a topic of conversation, nor did it occur to me that it might be a matter requiring negotiation in an intimate relationship. Extended discussions about what my deafness might mean for either me, or for them, or for the quality of our relationships simply did not happen. The men with whom I got romantically involved did not take the initiative to inquire either through misplaced sensitivity, or because they didn't know what they needed to understand, or because (as one former boyfriend recently owned up to me) "I didn't realize you were deaf when I first met you and then after a few days of knowing you, it just didn't seem relevant to us. It still doesn't."

I tossed aside the occasional jarring note as just "one of those things." As something that life throws up at you sometimes. As something to put up with. I flinched if, on missing what they said and asking them to repeat it, they answered, "Oh, it doesn't matter. It wasn't important," and turned away from me. They complained when I pretended to understand what was being said when I clearly did not. My smiles, intended to cover my incomprehension, apparently did not hide the blankness in my eyes. They would probe me then, their own frustration showing, "Doesn't what I say matter to you?" Of course it did. The question flustered me. Their words, all the ones I didn't hear as well as the ones I did hear, mattered a lot to me, but I could never break free of the double-edged sword of asking them to repeat their words, because . . . well, you know by now what would happen: they would say, "Oh, it doesn't matter. It wasn't important," and so the circle of uncertainty would continue, around and around again.

With this experience behind me, Damian's novel insistence on understanding my deafness pressed my buttons. His questions were searching; I understood them to mean that he was searching to understand me; it was seductive. When he withdrew his friendship from me, I felt terribly exposed, because in talking about my deafness with Damian in a way that I had not done with any other man, I had gathered up the daring to also talk about other matters, and . . . and what? I did not know what to think; it was confusing. I knew that Damian had not left me because of my deafness, but I did want to know if, and how, my deafness affected my relationships with men beyond the practical considerations of speaking up, speaking clearly, speaking face to face. There was an elephant in the room and I wanted to know its message.

When I thought about it a bit more, I decided that my deafness did not have much to do with my being single. After all, several of my friends were single, and they weren't deaf. Wasn't there some statistic about meteors and single women and available men?

On the other hand, that statistic didn't automatically rule out the possibility that my deafness was irrelevant to my single status, did it? And actually, a memoir on deafness I had read, the one by Bainy Cyrus, claimed that the success rate of marriages between deaf women and hearing men was pretty low. Really low. That was discouraging. Then again, I had only ever dated hearing men; why was that? Why had I never seriously considered the prospect of dating deaf men? (Leaving aside, for the time being, that I rarely met *any* single, available men let alone had the opportunity to apply the deaf/hearing filter to that particular gene pool.)

I remembered something else, something my mother had said to me when I was sixteen. I was going to school dances in church halls with the usual accoutrements of orange cordial, strobe lighting, and floorboards stamped in time to anthems such as "Peggy Sue," "Rock Around the Clock," "Will You Still Love Me Tomorrow?" "I Only Want to Be with You," and, of course, that end-of-night crowd pleaser, "Running Bear." The other girls looked keen in their miniskirts and boots, but the boys looked worried and their palms sweated during the close body-to-body sway of the slow dance songs. I was awkward with boys. I liked their company but could never really believe that they enjoyed my company in return, and so I embarked on the fatal course of feigning disinterest in the boys whom I liked enormously for fear of discovering their lack of interest in me. I thought the boys who chatted with me were being kind rather than sincere. I also hid my hearing aid as best as I could beneath my long hair, even as I wondered why I was doing this: after all, I would be "outed" eventually (and probably sooner rather than later). My lack of confidence meant that I spent a lot of time hanging around the perimeter of the hall or in the women's toilet chatting with my friends, spinning out the evening as best I could. Sometimes, I would sit outside the dance hall alone in the cool moonlight air to get relief from the press of noise and strain of pretense, and wonder when romance would enter my life.

After one such evening, I walked into my parents' bedroom and chanced a question that was on my mind. "Do you think that my being deaf has anything to do with boys not asking me out?" My father tilted his head reflectively but my mother's reply was immediate. "Rubbish! Standing around with a long face stops boys. Look cheerful and you'll be right."

I tried to be cheerful now by practicing gratitude. The twentieth anniversary of Jack's death was upon me, and I called Jack's father. This took some doing. We had parted on good terms when I left Australia for England four years earlier, but we had not been in contact with each other since then. I tracked him down, and a short while later, we met in a cafe near the riverside Botanical Gardens, where he explained that he did not want to take part in a commemorative ceremony. He liked the idea of it, understood that I saw it as an opportunity for healing, but said that he preferred to deal with the anniversary privately with his own family.

With that sorted out, we reminisced about our son over our coffees. We smiled wryly at some of our memories, as if Jack was still very much present in our lives. Jack's father talked about his work as an investor of sorts and his new family, a subject I greeted with guarded interest, and I told him about my "deaf project," which he responded to with gusto. I was startled by his enthusiasm. "That's great! You must do this. Absolutely." He nodded vigorously. "People will be really interested in it." I didn't press him further about this: what hurts or mysteries or doubts—or even joy, pride and humor—about my deafness had he nursed during our life together? Later, I wished I had asked him. Why didn't I? Again, what was I afraid of?

I went ahead with the ceremony to commemorate Jack's life one Sunday in early June, after mass with Father Adrian. I wanted to acknowledge not just my loss but also the loss to my family, especially my nieces and nephews who had held Jack too. I gave them each a polished marble egg with the word "love" or "joy" etched into it, and thanked them for their support all these years. Organizing such a ceremony outside the stock-standard Catholic rites was unusual in my family; it was a one-off event. We blushed, muttered, and shuffled our feet as we stood around the altar. My mother looked stern in her effort to hold in her emotions. Cecily chewed the inside of her cheek. My youngest nephew, Alex, grinned help-lessly. My eldest nephew, Jason, his eyes raised heavenward, examined the church ceiling as if assessing its sturdiness. My niece, Jessica, searched for a place to rest her gaze. Chris, my brother-in-law, thumped me on the shoulder afterward and said, "That was bloody terrific." Heartfelt.

The passage of time lulled me into feeling strong. I called Damian. This was a mistake. He answered the phone with a voice vibrating with fatigue, but on hearing my greeting, he chattered brightly for a few minutes before descending into the dulled tones of depression as he struggled to explain, again, his decision to remain apart from me. In the way that these things happen, we talked for longer than was helpful for either of us. When I said, "I don't know how to end this conversation," he answered, "No. I don't either." We held our silence together for several moments before one of us—it might have been me; it might have been him—said, "I'll call you in a couple of weeks. Maybe have coffee?" I pressed the dead handset to my forehead and could not find any gratitude within me at all.

I spilt the beans. I spoke of my heartache to friends and listened to their counsel as they poured themselves another glass of wine or cup of tea in my kitchen, or lit up their cigarettes on my balcony. Gerard was frantic on my behalf; his dark eyes brimmed with anxiety, "You've got to keep trying! Go back to him! Keep talking!" But most of my friends counseled otherwise.

"Detach. Move on."

"Remember the nice times you had with him."

"I bet he's a Gemini. You can never trust a Gemini."

"It's just bad timing."

"Keep your heart open to love."

These words made sense during their utterance—even the crack about the flightiness of Geminis—but the wisdom always died before it could reach my heart. I floundered; I knew what I had to do but sank deeper into my melancholy with each passing day. Rose rang. Our friendship had been forged during our university years when we wandered around the campus together and spent our long summer breaks hitchhiking through New Zealand or getting lost in the grand cities of Europe. We were witness to each other's twanging grief during times of unwise love. She got down to brass tacks. "Distract yourself with work," she said, her gentle voice doing nothing to mask her firmness of intent with me, "And do one nice thing for yourself each day."

It was easy to take the first piece of advice. As usual, I had a heavy schedule of work deadlines. This time, I was racing against the clock to write a short book about guardianship for the Queensland Law Reform Commission. I forced myself to be grateful for the distraction as well as the income, but my soul was not in it, and so, as soon as I could, I took up Rose's second piece of advice. I returned to Bethel to be comforted by the routines of silence in the retreat by the sea. There, I renewed my zest for my "deaf project." My heartache, while eased, took longer to be healed.

9

In the Beginning Was the Word

When I say out loud the words, "the retreat by the sea," I hear a dreamy singsong rhythm. They carry the beat of a nursery rhyme that a parent might tell her sleepy child, her head at rest on her pillow. I felt at rest at Bethel. The salt air, white sand, and blue shiver of the Pacific Ocean all cast their magic spell, but the most magical thing of all was the silence of companionship. The days of silence demanded a certain discipline for most hearing people, but I slid into it like a warm bath. The relief of moving among a group of people entirely unimpeded by the expectation that I would have to be on guard for sounds, watch for the direction in which they came from, decipher them, and respond to them by listening, speaking, laughing, or whatever was required of me was in itself restorative.

But the real gift of that silence lay in sharing it for five whole days and five whole nights with other people. I loved this. I loved eating my meals, reading the retreat literature, writing in my journal, watching the sea, and sitting alongside twenty other people all held in the spell of a companionable silence. I knew the silence of unwelcome aloneness and crushing loneliness, that drenching silence of melancholy; knew also the silence imposed by grief and terror; and the silence of guilt and anxiety too, of holding secrets that cannot be told. There's another silence; the silence of magnificence, the sort that forces wordlessness upon you on contemplating the grandeur of landscape; I had fallen victim to this awe during a visit to Central Australia where the red dirt, dappled with violet and yellow wildflowers, stretched into infinity to meet nothing but the glare of sky. The Bethel silence of companionship held none of this. It was the silence of comfort breaking into joy.

I was familiar with the idea of silent spiritual retreats, having gone to a Catholic girls' school; an annual retreat was part of the school calendar. Back then, my friends and I enjoyed them as a pleasant break from the classroom schedule. We whiled away the days by reading our Victoria Holt and Susan Howatch novels slipped in between the pages of books about Italian girls made saints for choosing death over the loss of their virginity—Maria Goretti's name sticks in my mind; why we were not taught how to defend ourselves against assault is beyond comprehension. God was not a high priority in my reflections during my school years. I didn't think much about God at all, to be honest. Not even when I went to Mass on Sundays or to the Benediction service on the first Friday of each month in the school chapel. And not even when I was in the Sodality of the Children of Mary which I was keen about because I fancied wearing the blue cape over my white dress. I liked going to these services for the same reason as I liked going anywhere. It was a change in the day-to-day routines; something interesting might happen; and if nothing new happened, then I had won some quiet time for myself. I also liked the hymns. Much of what the priests said sailed over my head. I thought about good and bad, and strove to do the right thing, but my thinking was inchoate.

I was jolted into trying to think more crisply when, just a month after the Bethel retreat, I heard a nun speak at a conference in Sydney. Her topic was the Gospel of John and its opening verse: "In the beginning was the Word, and the Word was with God, and the Word was God." A robust, bosomy and wholesome-looking woman in her fifties, she emphasized the beat of the words by slicing the air with one hand in time to their pulsing rhythm. She told how, in a society in which few people read and so relied on the traditions of oral storytelling, the early Christians needed to hear the word of God if they were to learn about God. It was regarded as an important part of their humanity. I drifted off, mulling over how deaf people developed their spirituality in the absence of hearing.

I had been prepared for my first Holy Communion and first Confession when I was six years old by attending classes at the local convent. My mother picked me up from the Deaf School each afternoon and drove me to those classes for several weeks. I could not remember how my presence was explained to the other six-year-old children in that convent class. Was my deafness explained to them? Who did the explaining and how was it done? Whatever the process, it must have been satisfactory enough. I still had my catechism notebook from those days. In it were the standard catechism questions and answers written in the dogged handwriting of a child, all illustrated with my crayon drawings and pictures of angels, saints, nativity scenes, and miracle after miracle. The Nativity. The Last Supper. The Resurrection. Ascension Thursday. The Assumption of Mary into heaven. My mother had helped me with the rote learning by changing some of the words. She had evidently thought about how to change conceptual words into "doing" words to guide me through my early religious instruction. "Question" was replaced by "ask" and "answer" had been replaced by "tell." Some of the questions and answers came back to me as I sat in the conference room that day. I could hear the singsong of six-year-old girls and boys chanting to the black-robed nun standing in front of the blackboard with its inscription *AMDG (All My Duty for God)* in the top right-hand corner:

Ask: Who made the world?

Tell: God made the world.

Ask: Why did God make me?

Tell: To know Him and love Him and to be happy.

Ask: How can I know God?

Tell: By learning about God.

And then the penny dropped. I came to, sat up straighter in the conference auditorium, leant forward, and paid more attention to the nun's lecture. She was also saying that people needed to see God as well as hear His Word. She seemed to have a thing about sight and sound. I could not follow her argument. What I did understand in that telescoping moment was this: historically, people's capacity for spirituality was understood to be an essential part of their humanity. If they did not have God in their lives, they were not fully human. I trembled. It was the first time that I grasped the historical aversion for deafness: deaf people could not hear; without hearing they could not know God; without knowing God, deaf people could not be human. It was crude logic, wasn't it? Awful. And what's more, I believe that a quiver of that prejudice remains today, two thousand years after John wrote his gospel.

I left that session in a distracted state. I had to give a paper immediately after lunch. Mine was about how writers write about silence, and what that meant for how stories of deaf people are told. I burned with what I had just learnt. I saw that my immediate task was to stay calm and to use my presentation to shake at least some of the conference participants' notions of what it means to be deaf. Perhaps I was not as calm as I aimed to be; the small audience of twelve academics and researchers was transfixed from my first opening salvo: "I'm deaf and I'm here to talk with you about stories of deaf people and what they might mean to you." An occasional nod showed me that people were responding to my words. One woman watched me with such intensity that I doubt that she even blinked. She came up to me after I finished speaking: "Do you know, in all my years of teaching literature in universities, I have never heard anyone give a paper about deafness in literature?"

I nodded, and said, "I can well imagine. That's my point. Stories of deafness have to travel out beyond disability and medicine into the world of novels and films. We learn about who we are as much by what we read and see about ourselves, as by what we are told and by what we experience." She gazed at me as if in a daze, grabbed my hands in a clasp, and then raced off to the next conference session. I felt breathless. I had broken through; *my* words had mattered. Conversations—if not conversions—begin with words.

Miracles. The New Testament reports that Jesus healed the lame, blind, and deaf. Charlatans in the nineteenth century sold potions in green glass bottles inscribed with the promise: "Cure for Deafness." When I was a little girl, an archbishop once splashed holy water from Lourdes onto my hearing aid and waved his hands in the sign of the cross over my head. No cure there. My nephew, Simon—the same one who wanted to be deaf— must have believed in miracles. Or perhaps he turned into a deaf-skeptic; if he wasn't allowed to be deaf, then why should I be allowed to be deaf? Picture this: Simon, still seven years old, pounding up the stairs at the back of his home. He's shouting.

"Mum, Mum! Donna's not deaf anymore!"

His mother is unmoved. She continues buttering the bread rolls for lunch. "Oh? Why do you say that?"

"Because she's in the pool, and, and, and (he's breathless; his excitement is overwhelming him), and she's swimming without her hearing aid on, and, and (significant pause here, juts his head forward), *She Can Understand What I'm Saying!*" He's triumphant. His face is alight. Even his freckles shine.

His mother turns to Simon, puts the butter knife down on the bench, eyes him, and says, "She can lipread you."

"Lipread me?"

"Yep, she doesn't have to hear you. She can understand what you're saying without her hearing aid."

"Oh."

Simon may have been disappointed, but I think this is quite a good miracle in itself.

Several months after that conference in Sydney, I read about Hall Caine's novel *The Scapegoat*, in which Israel, the Jewish hero, seeks the salvation of his daughter, Naomi, born deaf and blind. Israel establishes a routine of reading each night to his daughter, from the Book of the Law:

> Thus, night after night, when the sun was gone down, did Israel read of the law and sing of the Psalms to Naomi, his daughter, who was both blind and deaf. And though Naomi heard not, and neither did she see, yet in their

silent hour together, there was another in their chamber always with them—
there was a third, for there was God.[1]

I liked this assumption of God's presence in deaf-blind Naomi's life. I
felt that Hall Caine understood Naomi to be fully human, fully spiritual,
notwithstanding her inability to see and her inability to hear.

I had, by now, also read Helen Keller's memoir, *Story of My Life*, the
inspiration for the play and movie, *The Miracle Worker*. I came across that
famous scene of the young deaf-blind Helen at the well where she not
only discovers that words have meaning, but experiences this discovery as
a kind of intellectual and spiritual baptism. She wrote, "I knew then that
'w-a-t-e-r' meant the wonderful cool something that was flowing over
my hand. That living word awakened my soul." The trouble is that I do
not believe Helen Keller's account. Her reportedly "spontaneous" insight
smacks of a retrospective reshaping of events. Her "spiritual awakening"
seems overly adult. She was, after all, just a child at the time. I certainly
never experienced such a childhood awakening on discovering the spoken
word and its meaning.

The only childhood frisson about words that I can recall was when I
realized that I could lipread. I would have been five years old at the time
and still at the Gladstone Road School for the Deaf. I had not yet learned
my alphabet by rote, and so when the teacher called me to the front of the
class to recite it, I was anxious. I simply didn't know it, but then one of my
classmates, Matthew, started mouthing the letters to me. A. B. C. D. . .
Watching the movement of his lips, I repeated the letters with a fluency
that felt new to me. I still remember the relief of having "performed" successfully, but even this relief was not enough to awaken my soul.

As a child, I took everything for granted. I took my deafness for granted;
the gradual acquisition of language for granted; and the eventual total
immersion into the hearing world for granted. This is not to say that I was

---

1. Hall Caine 1853–1931. "The Scapegoat." Brian Grant. *The Quiet Ear: Deafness in Literature*. London: Deutsch, 1987, p. 117.

always sanguine. Not at all. Sometimes, I felt sad, lonely, separate from others, and confused, but I never questioned why this was so. I led a child's life; it was entirely unexamined. I simply accepted things and got on with the tasks of fitting in and adapting. I suppose, now, that over the years this may have resulted in my suppressing any overt exhibition of my sense of deaf-self. On the other hand, I developed the qualities of effort, tenacity, and perseverance.

10

The Best of Both Worlds

Now, all this reading was well and good, but it did not shine much light on how my deafness had shaped my own life. I was heated about some things, but I was not struck by an epiphany on my road to Damascus, nor zapped by a revelation of zigzag lightning clarity.

If anything, some of my reading reinforced my antagonisms about the hearing world's distorted understanding of deafness. I had encountered, for the first time, the shocking phrase "passing as hearing" in an essay by the esteemed American disability studies scholar Thomas Couser. When I kept seeing the same phrase in other books by different writers, I picked up the feeling that the hearing person feels tricked in some way, perhaps even resentful that deaf people don't carry an emblem like the white cane of blind people or the bell of the leper. It felt accusatory, but I didn't understand what the accusation was.

I was already used to the other accusation, the sneering one when someone calls out, "Hey! Are you deaf or something?" As if it's a crime to be deaf. Here was a new crime, but what was it? Did I stand accused of complying too well with the demands of the hearing world? Speak clearly, don't make funny faces when you speak, don't use your hands to speak, just sit quietly, don't draw attention to yourself by the way you speak, just watch, observe, listen, conform, comply. All these demands rushed to the surface of my being when I read "deaf passing as hearing." Years of effort, hurt, and resentments swelled in my heart. I wanted to scream at this writer, Thomas Couser. In fact, in the quiet of my lounge room, I *did* cry out. "Oh, for God's sake!" I felt trapped by the accusation of this man who had, at that time, never met me and did not know me. I couldn't be deaf because it irritates people. I couldn't be hearing because, well, I'm deaf. What *could* I be then?

Couser had written, "The desire of some deaf individuals to pass as hard of hearing, if not as hearing, suggests the continuing power of the stigma attached to deafness." Without disputing the power of stigma, I take exceptional issue with Couser's claim that "passing as hearing" is the deaf person's deliberate desire to hide his or her deafness, when what is more likely to be the case is that most deaf people just do not go about their daily lives thinking about their deafness. Hearing people can place undue emphasis on how deaf people feel about their deafness. Certainly, some hearing people might find an encounter with a deaf person in some way confronting, but it does not necessarily follow that all deaf people must find their own deafness confronting. They don't; *I* don't.

The phrase "deaf passing as hearing" is also said with the certainty that it means something. But what *does* it mean? Is it meant to signify that the deaf person must always proclaim, announce, call out her deafness as her trump card of identity? Or is it meant to signify that the deaf person who speaks well, who is oral, and who does not inject her conversations with repetitive alerts of "I may be oral but I am also deaf" is, in fact, a fake? Such an accusation is not only unimaginative, it is cruel. People who might use the term "passing as hearing" cannot have it both ways. For so long as sign language is marginalized as a "second language" rather than universally accepted as a companion language to the individual's native language (such as English, Spanish, Italian, and so on), then deaf people are required to communicate orally with hearing people as best as they can. It is unjust then, to turn on that deaf person and implicitly accuse her of fraud.

Most deaf people go out of their way to avoid seeing signs of impatience on hearing people's faces—the eyes rolled toward heaven, the whitening of the stretched upper lip line, the flared nostril as they seethe with their irritation at having to repeat what they've said because the deaf person missed it the first time. We tolerate the studied tolerance of "Would. Madam. Like. Help?": the rounded vowels delivered in a slow hand-clap time by the sales assistant who has attended a Deaf Awareness Seminar and spotted the hearing aids beneath the tuck of hair. We learn to keep our cool in the face of the crudely cast question, "Why do you talk like that?" And yet still, deaf people must face this accusation of "deaf passing as hearing."

And what does it mean to "be deaf"? I am constantly struck by the low level of awareness about the diversity of deaf experiences. It is as if deaf people are allowed only one image. And what might that image be? The deaf and dumb person, the deaf-mute person, or the person who makes "animal-like noises"?

Despite my anger about all this, I didn't feel *transformed* by my reflections so far. Keen as ever to allay parents' fears, yes. More assertive about claiming my deafness, yes, most definitely. But, transformed and enlightened? No. And nor was there any improvement in the quality of my romantic love life, if that was any yardstick to go by.

Something happened. Something exciting. I discovered Sandra, that little girl with the red hair at the Gladstone Road Deaf School who had so inspired my mother all those years ago. I found her on my laptop.

Bored with myself, I had gone in search of other deaf people who might also be asking questions about deaf identity. A friend suggested that I write to a fellow he knew in Melbourne; he was deaf too and was writing a book about his experiences as one of three deaf children   his parents and one of his sisters were hearing. His name was Michael. And so I wrote to Michael, I e-mailed him. He e-mailed back. I replied to his e-mail, and before I knew it, we had settled into a rhythm of almost weekly correspondence, swapping bits and pieces of our life stories, as much as we dared to reveal in our separate cocoons of not-knowing-each-other. I was hair-trigger cautious; I didn't want to be "Damian-ed" all over again. We trod safe waters, told each other what we were reading and the stories we wanted to tell the world. He wrote, "I have a soft spot for David Wright [the South African deaf poet whose memoir I had turned my back on], because it was the first time I had ever read anyone attempting to tell what it was like to be deaf." Michael, a journalist and disability advocate, had the gift of inquiry and he was generous with me in sharing his knowledge, ideas, and discoveries. He had spent much of his adult life asking questions about deafness and deaf people's lives—his pet project was Henry Lawson, a nineteenth-century Australian writer and poet who was deaf as a result of a childhood illness—and on finding answers that he didn't like, answers that played to prejudices and stereotypes, he would take them on. His e-mail stories to me about his battles were cheerful and full of good humor, but his doggedness showed through, as did his research.

Michael led me to the group of deaf academics who corresponded with each other on the Internet. When I logged on to find them, I saw that they were from all over the world. Finland. Japan. Saudi Arabia. Netherlands. Canada. England. Ireland. North America. This excited my curiosity; the northern hemisphere was evidently a hothouse of deaf talent. I was also terribly impressed by the scale of their achievements. These deaf academics held bachelor's and master's degrees and doctorates in child psychology, agriculture, literature, medicine, science, theology, philosophy, education. The honors list was long. They were experienced researchers, lecturers, teachers, writers, and thinkers. I recognized some names by their literary reputations and noted that several other names popped up often during e-mail flurries. Susan De Gaia was a regular correspondent. She wrote, "Analysing the way stories are told can show us a lot about who is most powerful, most heard, whose perspective matters most to society. I think if we polled deaf/Deaf people, we would find many things missing from the stories that are told about them." The lengthy e-mail exchanges covered topics as random as phantom sounds, biblical stories about deafness, music (cyberspace was noisy on this subject; several deaf academics wrote with detailed descriptions of their joy for song, dance, and musical instruments along with their bemusement at hearing people's bemusement about that joy), and inevitably, that evergreen issue—the debate about signing and oralism. Many of them wrote of their reliance on sign language, and of their wish for its greater acceptance and support. I followed the trail of these discussions in the night quiet of my study, illuminated only by the bluish-white glare radiating from the laptop screen. Their sense of community was strong; immense distances separated them, but they wrote with a casual familiarity with each other, as if they were kicking around a ball together at the local park. I didn't take part. Diffidence held me back. What did I have to say that was new or clever or perceptive? I was a novice in the deaf identity debate. Besides, I was an oral deaf person; I fell into that sometimes-disparaged category of "not deaf enough." Would I be welcomed into this diaspora of deaf academics? I didn't know.

And then one Sunday night, the first paragraph of an e-mail in these exchanges snagged my attention. It said, "I believe personal story-telling is essential in understanding the diversity of our deaf situations, and learning to respect our differences within the d/Deaf umbrella. Basically, these are 'being-in-the-world experiences.'" Aha, I thought. This writer was treading across the same ground as I was. She had a lot she wanted to say about her deaf experiences, but was unsure of her right to say it. She was going to mark out her rightful claim simply by recounting her personal experiences. I liked her instincts. I read on. And as I read on, goosebumps tingled up and down my arms. My excitement rose as if I was a child lost in a fairy tale. This writer—I jumped down to the bottom of her e-mail to check her name, Sandi, before reading on; the name didn't register—wrote that she could

recall my own school situation when I was put into the first oral deaf class in Brisbane (in Queensland, Australia) in the 50s, firstly in the Deaf School, where the oral deaf class was segregated carefully from the signing deaf children. We were put into a tiny little room in an old building, far away from the main building where the signing deaf children were allocated. We had different lunch times, to ensure there were no contacts with signs, and then we were moved to a small Oral Deaf school.

Not long after that, I was sent to a mainstream class situation (as an "experiment"). It was a shock to my system going from a tiny class of 9–10 deaf children to a huge class of 43–45 hearing children! Of course, I had no choice but to try to work within the system. One of the strategies I learnt was to talk with the teacher about how I would benefit from learning in the hearing class, as I was lip-reading totally at that time. Interpreters were unheard of in those days. I would always sit at the front, with one child taking turns each term to sit with me, to write down notes for me, and to explain (mouthing the words) anything I missed during the sessions. It was a system that worked very well for me, as we both learned very quickly—the hearing student "double-learning" and the deaf student absorbing information. If there were problems, I'd check with the teacher. I think being young children, we were flexible with the learning, so it was a very good system for me within the hearing situation. This was okay as long as I had one teacher for the whole year, as I got used to lip-reading him or her.

High school was very different with six different subjects and six different lip-reading patterns to learn, plus all the other lips in the classes! I learned to adapt my strategies, and was fortunate with one student sticking with me for most subjects the whole school duration. That student received excellent grade marks from the "double learning," and I benefited as well. I cannot remember being lonely or isolated at school, but I do remember "fighting" for my right to learn, though at that time (in the 60s) I didn't know about "rights." I believe it was a subconscious way to "survive" within a system that I had to deal with.

I was gobsmacked.

Was this my twin sister separated at birth or what? No. Our experiences may have been the same, but this woman had had more guts than me. Not in a million years would I have had the nerve to "talk with the teacher about how I would benefit from learning in the hearing class." I grinned at this; I read this line several times. It really took my fancy. I thought about how terrific it would have been to have "Sandi" with me at All Hallows to "talk with the teacher." She would have stood up to that teacher, Miss Morrison, in Grade Four, who repeatedly sent me to the back of the class-room for being "disruptive." This because I dared to ask the girl next to me, Julie, to tell me what Miss Morrison was saying; her back was always turned to the class; she was either wilful, stupid, or lazy in her refusal to face me when she spoke. I knew enough not to talk back to her. I would fiddle with my hearing aid instead, hoping this charade would alert her, remind her of my circumstance. No. She played dumb. I would walk to the back of the class, avoiding the girls' eyes. My difficulties with this teacher must have shown up in my schoolwork; I was pulled out of her class for one afternoon every week for several weeks—I don't remember now for how long—to go to the Deaf School for some sort of educational "top-up." I didn't really mind this. It was a relief to be out of Miss Morrison's way. My chief grumble about going back to the Deaf School was that I had to go to the "Big School" at Annerley, where it was dark and dingy, and where I didn't know any of the other children. I would have relished going back to the Gladstone Road Deaf School, where I might have met up with my old classmates. Sharon. Kay. Matthew. I lamented. Sandi, where were you when I needed you? And then, "Sandi"?

I turned my attention back to the laptop keyboard, wrote a short note introducing myself, and asked in closing, "I wonder if you are the same Sandra who was a year or so older than me with red hair? And you were taught by Mr. Bellagoi? Fingers crossed in anticipation."

When I was at the Deaf School, I didn't see myself as being "a deaf child with special needs." Even though I was being taught about sound and how to speak, I must have assumed—if I gave it any thought at all, which is unlikely—that this was how everyone learned to speak, that this was what everyone did at school. I understood myself to be deaf and different only after I was switched from a school for deaf girls and boys to a private girls' school that had no deaf children, All Hallows. I cannot remember if I was consulted about this move; perhaps I was, perhaps not. (Were seven-year-old children consulted on such serious matters in those days? Or is the practice of consulting children about major decisions a latter-day development?) What I do remember is that I seem to have gone through the motions of this move in a dreamy, fuguelike state. One day, I was in the Deaf School's grey uniform with maroon trim and distinctive smell of newly ironed gabardine, and the "next day" (actually, it would have been eight weeks later, at the end of the summer holidays), I was in a new martial brown uniform with box pleats and more buttons than anyone could possibly need. I was pleased to get a new uniform but didn't think too deeply about what it meant.

At this school with no other deaf children, I was slow to understand that it was *I* who was different. I was so dazzled by the newness of this convent school, with the nuns in their black robes and white wimples creasing their foreheads, and by the noise and chattiness of the other girls, that I thought that *they* were different. In the first few days, I watched them all from the angle of observing *their* difference. But when my new classmates eventually gathered up the boldness to ask their tumbling questions about my hearing aid and about my speech, I finally understood. *I* was the object of curiosity. When the reality finally broke through the clouds of my foggy comprehension that I had left my old school for this one, I cried a few mornings on arriving at the new school. I told my teacher, Sister Mary Eugenia, that my head ached. The nun must have rung my parents, because my father then drove me to school each morning for a while until the realization settled within me that this was it; I was here to stay.

Photos of me from that time show me standing at attention in the back yard, in my uniform with straw hat and brown gloves, Globite bag in hand. My old grey uniform with maroon trim was folded away in a bottom drawer. Each morning, my mother combed my long hair tightly back off my face into a ponytail, revealing my hearing aid with its pink cord looping its way from my left ear to inside the collar of my uniform down to the bulge near my waist. The box of sound pressed warmly against my flesh, the up-down volume button rustling against the cloth of my uniform. I would try to loosen my hair so that it covered my ears; but no, the band was fastened securely. "Mum, it's too tight, my ears stick out." I would pull at the ribbons, mussing up my hair. Cecily, watching this, chewed her bottom lip in sympathy. My mother would call out: "Leave it; let everyone see your beautiful ears!" She wanted to send me off to my new school with the rhythm of bravado in my footsteps: I was deaf; I wore a hearing aid; that was that. I was doubtful, this wasn't a good idea. I wanted my hair falling loose, the way it had been before.

I seethed to my mother about the girls' questions. "Answer the questions, just tell them. They aren't being unkind, they just want to know, that's all." My mother was brisk. But I cried, my voice breaking: "They ask me all the time!" My deafness acted as a magnet for my new classmates. "Why do you talk like that? Why can't you say 'ess'? Why can't you sit with me at the back of the class? Why can't, why not, why . . .?" I could not find a way to satisfy the thirst of my questioners; little girls themselves, they were unable to contain their voyeurism. I especially hated the shy, sly requests to look at my hearing aid, not just the metal box tucked away under my pleated school uniform but the ear-mould too. The gaze of so many eyes brought the girls too close to me, as if they were peering into my very ears. I was ashamed too because—and this shame was unspeakable—my ear-mould invariably held traces of yellow-brown crusty earwax caught in the curve of their ridges, just like grains of sand caught inside seashells, but without the romance of the sea. I wished my ear-mould could look shiny.

At best, my answers gave me fragile cover; at worst, they opened the door to more frightening questions. "Why can't you hear? Did you do something wrong?" The accusation twanged, swelled to a roar, and soared like a loosed arrow to its target. The "something" part of the question glanced off my cheek but the "wrong" bit pierced my chest. I sucked in air, searched my questioner's face for cruelty, but saw only a freckled face knotted with the wanting to know. I coughed up my answer, trying to catch my breath. "I was just born that way. I was born deaf. You know, I was just born," stumbling now, "not to hear." The last words felt clumsy in my mouth, took up too much room, stretched my lips unnaturally. I backed away into the shadow of a doorway. "I didn't do anything wrong," my voice faltered. "There's nothing wrong." Even as I repeated the words, I felt queasy. I was not sure.

I didn't think the girls were being deliberately cruel; they were too consistently cheerful and willing, in the way of all little girls with ribbons in their hair and short socks crinkling around their ankles, to enfold me into their skipping games and ring-around-the-rosy for me to fall prey to that notion. It was more that I found their curiosity baffling. After all, I didn't ask them about their hearing, did I? Why were they being such stickybeaks? It was rude, that's what it was. Rude. Besides, I didn't know *how* to answer their questions. They were practical girls. Mechanically minded.

"How does your hearing aid work?"

"Why do you talk like that?"

"What can you hear?"

I didn't know the answers to these questions. Why would I? I just put my hearing on each morning and took it off each evening; I wasn't ripping the back off the metal case to find out how it worked. And what did they mean by "talk like that"? How was I talking? I sounded all right, didn't I? No one had ever commented to me on my voice before. What was I saying differently now? (Apart from that awful "ess" sound; I knew I couldn't do that one; would never do it.) And what could *they* hear? How could I answer such a question? How did anyone describe what they could and could not hear? Why couldn't they settle down and leave me alone and just go along with things? What's with all these questions! They rained down like Hitchcock's black birds swooping down on Tippi Hedren. I tried to answer the girls in a way that maintained my eight-year-old dignity and stalled their curiosity. The torrent of questions eventually subsided; a renegade one would surface every now and then, but I never ever again experienced such an intrusion of peering into my ears, my sounds, myself.

I was exercised by the challenge of interpreting the whirl of sounds around me in the classroom and playgrounds, my teachers and classmates swinging from face-contorting exaggerated clarity of speech to forgetting to face me so that I could see what was being said. I worked hard to be "normal," to be invisible inside the wider group around me. Despite the effort required of me, I had no sense of injustice about this. Instead, I accepted that it was my task—with hurts and all—to fit into this new world that had no other deaf children. I was compliant. After a while, I collected new names to remember: Susan, Maria, Julianne, Dianne, the twins Deborah and Phillepeau. The girls enjoyed my quietness and the intensity of my gaze on their faces. They mistook this for a fascination with their conversation, not knowing my fatigue from the effort of comprehending quick words, of catching sentences slipped through murmuring lips, of watching for nuances of impatience as I missed their meaning. My smiles disguised my lapses of concentration. I longed for the carefully spaced words of my old teachers at the Deaf School; I missed the theater of my conversations with my old friends, their faces lively with meaning and their hands gesturing the story when their words could not. I was school-sick: I didn't want to learn any more new names. I liked the old ones: Sharon, Matthew, Kay, Jenny. I had not said goodbye to Sharon, my best friend, because I had not understood that I was leaving her. I still did not grasp it. I wondered when I would go back to my old school; how long was I going to be at this new school? I did not want to ask my mother. Somehow, such a simple direct question was beyond my grasp.

Even a year after I started at my new school, when I was nine years old and in grade four, I sometimes stood at the cross-wire fence bordering the playgrounds and imagined that I could see across the muddy river to the Deaf School. I wasn't unhappy, but I felt tense and on guard; I was in the wrong place. I didn't belong at the new school; I belonged at the Deaf School. On the first day of each new school year for a few years, I would wait, looking out with hope for Sharon with her shy smile and hair tied back into a ponytail. I never expressed my hope aloud to anyone: I kept it to myself. Somehow I knew the voicing of this hope out loud would clang. It would jar in a way that I did not understand. Instead of killing the hope swiftly by exposing it, I secured it to myself for too many years, allowed the hope to wilt a little more each year. I lost a little bit of heart.

It took me the rest of my primary school years before I accepted that I was staying at All Hallows and made real efforts to belong. In grade seven, I went about the business of making new friends, "recruiting" them by just asking, "Will you be my friend?" Despite its bluntness, this was a surprisingly effective technique. Over time, I learned through closer observation that the art of friendship was subtle. It lay in the ebb and flow of exchanges among the girls, which could be cryptic, involving as they did the codes of adolescence along with a lot of aimless hanging around beneath the eaves of the classroom windows or in the shade of the trees on the terraced lawns. I hung around, grew more involved in school life, and made friends.

I walked to the bus stop each afternoon with Roslyn and Maria; went to the movies with Susan and Angela; stayed over at Michelle's home on the other side of the city; took off on beach holidays with Janeane; and bantered with Marion and Charmaine, making us all laugh outside our English and History classes.

In hindsight, it doesn't seem possible, but my deafness was rarely commented upon during my high school years, either by my friends or by my teachers. Their efforts to accommodate my needs must have been subtle, instinctive, or random, and I avoided making a public display of asserting my deafness. My friends may have commented on my deafness among themselves; I have no idea, but if they did, I never suffered any untoward splashback. If anything, they sometimes went out of their way to make sure I caught what they were saying. I knew by the occasional awkward silence or sidelong glances among the other girls when I was missing out on the nuances of their conversations, but not to any degree that bothered me (or them, apparently). I lived with the knowledge that a thin membrane of incomprehension separated me from everyone else. When I did feel uncomfortable, I sat quietly until the discomfort passed. Like a suppressed burp. My teachers presumably shared their observations among themselves. I muddled through and certain things were taken for granted: I always sat at the front of the classroom, and the teachers always faced the class when they spoke (no more of that Miss Morrison nonsense). On the other hand, I was not cut any slack in my studies: I had to take part in the oral French language classes with Madame Bougeais, along with the rest of my classmates. I was mutely appalled by this, but as things turned out, I learned to speak high school French adequately; the repetitive mimicry required to master any new language suited my learning style. I studied hard and did well in my subjects, joined the school magazine committee, and signed up for everything that was going to assert my place in the world. Each achievement bolstered my confidence.

My competence was a double-edged sword. Somehow, sometime—I don't know how or when—my deafness subsided into a state of visible invisibility. I knew I was deaf; everyone around me knew I was deaf; but I was silent about my dance back and forth across that border of hearing-deaf that marked out our differences, a border that was permeable but permanent. For no particular reason that I can recall (other than this was at a time when it was not "done" to talk about oneself), I felt inhibited about speaking about my deafness or describing what I might need to make things easier for myself. Instead, I made a point of smiling a lot, of looking cheerful, to cover my paddling-duck efforts to keep up. This was evidently thin cover: one afternoon as we were packing up our books at the end of a class, Ann, who was audacious enough to wash her hair in henna-dye against all the prohibitions of the nuns and who sat next to me in Modern History, said, "You hide a lot, don't you? You act as though everything is easy for you, but . . ." She cocked her head at me as if daring me to challenge the truth of her words. I laughed off her observation. "You've caught me out!"

I finished school with high marks (my obsessive study habits paid off; actually, I shared first place in the final exams with my friend, Janeane, the one who liked "carpenters") and settled into university life in the same clouds of confusion, excitement, and exam terror as any other student. I was pleased to go to university because I wanted to be where my friends went, and that's where they were going. I didn't know what I wanted to do with my life and was merely filled with vague, ill-defined hopes. I flirted with the idea of being a poet after my sister introduced me to the Australian poet Val Vallis. I thought I could finance that occupation by being a journalist until it was put to me that I would have difficulty doing interviews, press conferences, and the like. The idea of being a lawyer then seemed the right thing to take on, but when I went to court one day to get a better feel for it, that idea went right out the window. I could not hear a single thing being said in the courtroom; didn't even know when people were speaking and fell into a swivel of head-turning in search of voices like a crazed homing pigeon. I would have liked to study to be a teacher but that option had been ruled out by the Department of Education: "No deaf people need apply" was their motto back then. Finally, I settled into that no-man's land of an Arts Degree before crystallizing my intentions to be a social worker.

University life was a mostly benign experience for me. My preoccupations were ephemeral rather than gritty; I was not inclined to the radical student life and could usually be seen in one of the libraries tackling my assignments (for example, "Describe how the bucolic ideal was reflected in Chinese culture during the T'ang Dynasty"; I had to look up the meaning of "bucolic"), or sitting in the refectory with my friends, talking about the new Ingmar Bergman film or workshopping the suitability (or not) of the boys in our lives. In all my years at university, I was only once confronted by the impact of my deafness in an incident that played itself out as farce.

In 1973, before the advent of antidiscrimination legislation, a university professor was so enraged to find me in her Japanese language school that she gave me a subject credit in Introduction to Japanese 101 halfway through the year just to be rid of me. She summoned me to her office to damn me. "Who do you think you are? Lowering the standard of my classes with your disgraceful diction! How dare you! You're *deaf!*" Pushing herself up from her chair, the professor leaned across her desk and banged both her knuckled fists on top of a pile of papers. I made a stammering attempt to protest, but her face was a pale Kabuki mask of fury with white-rimmed lips. She scared me, and to be honest, part of me understood her point of view. I could not speak the Japanese language, and I was never going to be able to speak it properly despite hours each week in the language laboratory because I could not hear certain combinations of sounds specific to the Japanese language, such as "ts" as in "tsunami." (How do deaf Japanese people do it?) I had enrolled in first-year Japanese language because I was fascinated by the scrolling beauty of the Japanese script, the hiragana, katakana, and the kanji. I thought I would steer my way through at least one year by concentrating on the written elements of the language, and learn a little about Japanese culture and history along the way. My efforts to defend myself infuriated the professor. She sucked in her breath and heaved out her compromise in slow, drawn-out syllables designed to demonstrate her magnanimity: "If you attend all the lectures and the exams (*long pause*), just turn up for them (*longer pause*), I will arrange for you to be granted a credit pass. (*Lips drawn tight. Very tight.*) But you are never (*longest pause*), ever, to enroll in my course again." She collapsed back into her chair, exhausted. My face was hot and my heart seemed to be jumping around. I did not know what to think or what to feel. My friends showed me the way. "You lucky thing," they said.

Even though I was always pleased to hear news of my Deaf School friends through the grapevine, I did not seek them out in my early years at university. Without giving it too much thought at the time, I played out my life as a deaf person immersed in a hearing world. So much so that I bristled whenever anyone attempted to introduce me to another deaf person on the spurious grounds that we would "have so much in common." All my friends at university were hearing; none of us commented on my deafness (and I didn't comment on their hearingness). There was another girl in my first-year history tutorials who wore a hearing aid. I didn't regard her as being deaf though; I just saw her as having a hearing loss that needed to be remedied with a hearing aid. I have no idea why I came to this conclusion. Perhaps it was because I had never met her before, she was not one of my Deaf School friends. I rarely spoke with her, and she rarely spoke with me. Her speech was clipped and her gaze was cool. A tacit understanding lay between us; we were wary to the point of mutually civil hostility, and buried any curiosity we may have had about each other.

A couple of years later, during my third year at university, a friend invited me to move into her Highgate Hill apartment, which she shared with another girl, Bridget. Now, here's the rub: Bridget was losing her hearing at a rapid speed but I didn't think she was really deaf either! Some prejudice lay deep within me; apparently, only that particular group of people with whom I had shared my childhood days at the Deaf School were *really* deaf. Bridget and I enjoyed each other's friendship, but back then, I did not understand her response to her hearing loss, which was apparently to embrace the whole world of deafness, including signing and deaf theatre. In fact, I was shocked by it. I was shocked that she would turn her back on something that I had worked so hard for—the ability to communicate orally. Because we liked each other, we made tentative attempts to make sense of each other but let our efforts fade away into a glide of uncomprehending acceptance. (When I talked with Bridget about these times several years later, she shared her own perspective: "I didn't really *embrace* my deafness. I wouldn't use that word. It was more that I was very grateful for the help I was given by the deaf community. They gave me hope. I also got the impression that you felt threatened by my interest in the deaf world." On reflection, Bridget's intuition was right. I was uneasy about her interest in the deaf world; I did not want her to draw me into its culture.)

Bridget's hearing loss became profound over the years, and it politicized her, but I felt that her political response was based on a caricature of how a hearing person perceives the world of deafness, that is, as a community of signing deaf. Because my starting point was deafness, my life's task went in entirely the opposite direction: I embraced the hearing world, which was similarly based on a caricature of sorts, that is, my public hearing persona excluded the possibility of new deaf friendships and strained my loyalty to my old deaf friends. I did not explore the possibility of straddling both worlds, despite the occasional invitation to do so. When one of my childhood deaf friends visited me at my parents' home, out of the blue, and invited me to join him at the deaf theater, I could not muster the emotional flexibility that I felt this required. I did not have the confidence to embark on the swings and roundabouts of moving between the deaf community and my hearing family and friends. Instead, I let myself be content to hear news of my childhood deaf friends through the grapevine, but this was, inevitably, a patchy process that lent itself to distortion. Single snippets of information about this person or that person ballooned into portrait-size depictions of their lives as I sketched the remaining blanks of their history with my imagination as my only tool.

As the years rolled on, Bridget's life diverged so much from mine that we lost common ground. She went on to study at Gallaudet University in the United States and established herself back in Australia as a lecturer in deaf studies; I worked exclusively within the hearing world of government and public policy. It is tempting to conclude that we reversed our places: she, born hearing and then deafened as a young adult, found her place in the deaf community; while I, born deaf and then "hearingly" shaped by my education and upbringing, found my place in the hearing community.

However, this does us both a disservice, painting our lives too narrowly within deaf-hearing filters.

Six hours after I hit the "send" button of my e-mail to "Sandi," her reply popped up on my laptop screen. "Your 'anticipatory' fingers can uncross now. Yes, I remember you very well . . . who can forget you!" I smiled and read on, leaning in close as if to soak up each word in my heart's memory.

"Yes, I am the same Sandra with the red hair who was a year older than you, and yes, Mr. Belligoi was my teacher at Gladstone Road Oral Deaf School, also Mrs. Mason and Mr. Thomas. . . . Do you remember the ballet classes we used to do in the downstairs room?" and on she wrote for two pages, her every line charged with affection for the young deaf girls we once were. Her descriptions had the power of sepia photographs. I recalled everything she wrote about as if she were turning the pages of an old album—"the matron in her crisply starched white muslin head-scarf, her neatly pressed white uniform, with the small red cape around her shoulders, her stockings and polished shoes. She would smile while ushering us children toward the nurse for that big needle." Like me, Sandra's parents had encouraged her "to the highest possible attainment in education." She had gone on to a mainstream school, done well, and believed she had "received the 'best of both worlds' in the deaf and hearing education environments." Also like me, she had adopted a stance of self-sufficiency throughout her school years, and while "there was a lot of hard slog behind the scenes," she had "just merely worked hard in tackling problems as they surfaced."

Sandra's excitement in releasing her memories onto the page had a bouncing quality, as if she could not contain herself. It felt like a family reunion. We traded more than words with each other; more even than our memories. The two of us had been part of something special. We had both emerged from a particular time in history when our lives might so easily have been pulled more in one direction than the other.

A few weeks later, I met up for coffee again with Jennifer, my childhood friend from the deaf school and erstwhile Auslan teacher, who had once said to me, "When we were children, we were all like brothers and sisters. In some ways, we had more in common with each other, understood each other better than our family members." Jennifer had traveled a distance to come to my home, but I was tired from an unusually long bout of the flu and was not the lively company that I wanted to be for her. Our conversation faltered. Jennifer must have seen something flicker across my face; she was a perceptive woman. She asked me if I was in a romantic relationship or in love. I said no, and promptly mentioned Damian, giving a few details. Straight away, she said, "Oh, he has a lot of baggage. He has much sorting out to do." I was worn down, not by her words but by the truth of them. After Jennifer went home, I lay down on my bed. I thought that I would not leave my room again; I was extremely tired.

My tiredness was worryingly persistent. During this time of illness and restless nights in which my sleep was disrupted by night sweats, I went to several doctors. They mostly nodded a lot and wrote out prescriptions for antibiotics. The medication didn't help. I tore up the prescriptions and threw out the medication, opting to do longer morning walks instead, in an effort to build up my energy. I struggled with my work—in itself an unusual event—and wondered if I was depressed. An old school friend who was a doctor offered to monitor me for a few months: I accepted. Other angels of friendships flew into my life. They picked me up and carried me through weeks of comfort and joy filled with breakfast, lunch, and dinner invitations to their homes; with telephone conversations, visits, and e-mail hellos; with movies, restaurants, and art shows; with laughing and storytelling and love.

11

Work

Most people feel equivocal about their work. It's either good days peppered with bad days or, if you're unlucky, bad days that only occasionally give way to the good day here and there. I was one of the lucky ones. Despite all the tension of freelancing, worrying about where my next project would come from, and the clenched-teeth race to meet my deadlines, I enjoyed my work, and I liked my clients. I did not take either the work or the clients for granted, and so, when I kept falling ill with one thing after another in the long winter and into the spring, I did not see this as a chance to slow down, to take a break. Instead, I fretted about not working to my usual 24/7 intensity.

My capacity for work had always been a defining characteristic; it was ingrained in my DNA. At times of stress, work was my refuge. I didn't always like this. I often resented it. I shouted at my mother once. "Stop asking me about my work! I'm not a machine! Ask me about my friends! Ask me about my life!" When the shouting was done, I asked myself these questions instead and, in doing so, I thought of another question: how had my deafness shaped my professional life?

I was twenty-one years old when I started working in my first "real" job, as a recruitment clerk in the Australian Public Service Board. Now, there's a word that's not heard or seen much these days—"clerk." It has been replaced by grander titles such as "administrative assistant" or even "executive officer." After four years of part-time work, while I was studying at university, as a waitress and housemaid, neither of which I was good at despite my earnestness—I was chronically nervous in the first, would I understand what was being asked of me, said to me? and I was sloppy in the second, not mastering the art of tucking in those sheets hospital-bed-corner-style—I was relieved to get a proper job, in an office, doing things. So, here I was, a Clerk Grade 2/3, and my aspirations lay in being promoted to Clerk Grade 4. I didn't look beyond that. I had no great ambitions other than to be useful; I was also enrolled at university as a part-time social work student.

As it happened, I was shunted into a different professional stream and promoted instead to Assistant Research Officer and dispatched to the Defence Department in Canberra, where I was supposed to put my graduate knowledge of history together with my skills of research and analysis to use. This move came through the encouragement of good bosses. David was the manager of the recruitment services unit and George was my immediate supervisor; he had recruited me. Mr. Gordon Rainbow was "The Boss" and was always addressed by everyone as "Mr. Rainbow" or "The Boss." He was never "Gordon." Such informality was unthinkable back then. I opted for "Mr. Rainbow." One day, a colleague, Barbara, crooked her finger and signaled me to come over to her desk. I was in awe of her; she was older, perhaps even as old as thirty, with short black hair cut into a bob, and she was loud and confident. She looked like a career woman. I thought this was terrific. She also sat next to this fellow who I had a secret crush on despite his grumpy greetings to me each morning; Ian was his name. Anyway, Barbara called me over and, leaning toward me, said in a conspiratorial tone, "The Boss wants to see you." No explanation. Nothing. Just "The Boss wants to see you. Now." I was still new, had only been in the position of Clerk Grade 2/3 for a few months, and sweated at the prospect of going into the Boss's office. What had I done? Was I in trouble already?

Mr. Rainbow pulled a sheet of paper lying on his desk toward him. He waved me to a chair and smiled genially. He really was "genial." It's not a word that I would use of many people, but that word was made for Mr. Rainbow; his very name, redolent of the shine of colors against a dark sky, suited him. He looked over his glasses and spoke in tones of utmost kindness. "I have a letter here from the mother of a young man you interviewed recently. I see from her letter that her son has hydro-encephalitis." He looked up at me. "You remember him?" I nodded. How could I forget? The young man, eighteen years old, had impressed me. We had all sat in that small room with the glazed glass window shielding us from the curious glances of passing office workers—mother, son, and me in the role of Clerk Grade 2/3 interviewing prospective applicants for positions as clerical assistants (the bottom of the public service ranks) in the Taxation Department—and I had been self-conscious about the need to keep the expression on my own face looking restrained, nonchalant even, when all I really wanted to do was to stare at the moon-sized wobbling head in front of me. The mother looked sad, anxious, eager, protective, and proud of her son all at once. He looked calm. Accepting. Ready to accept whatever came his way. I didn't feel any sense of urgency or plea from him at all. I followed his cue, rather than his mother's, and conducted the interview.

The mother had written a letter of immense gratitude. It seemed that despite my horror for the young man—all through the interview, I had had a second conversation going through my mind, a conversation of sympathy for him—I had managed to focus all my questions on quizzing him about his abilities: What did he want to do with his life? What sort of work was he confident in doing? How did he see his career progressing? Apparently, I had asked him whether I thought his hydrocephaly would affect his work performance in any way, but had simply nodded in response to his answer (I cannot remember it) and moved on to the next question, and it was this that the mother was most grateful about. She had written that I was gentle and respectful to her son. Always courteous. I had even put them at their ease.

Mr. Rainbow beamed at me. His geniality glowed. He said, "Good work. Keep it up." And that was it. Our conversation was over. He'd read the mother's letter to me, smiled at me, and told me to "keep it up." I left his office ten feet tall, my heart thudding through my chest cartoonlike, and my face fire-engine red. I had never been praised for my work before. This was the first time I had ever been told that I had done a good job. And all because I'd been nice to a young man with a disability. That's how the mother and Mr. Rainbow apparently understood it. But I sensed something more. I knew that I had succeeded, not because of any innate qualities within me, but because I'd instinctively followed the young man's lead; *he* had been gentle, respectful, and courteous. He had laid down the ground rules for how the interview was to be conducted, and I had accepted his challenge. This all happened a very long time ago. The interview with the mother and son would have been done in thirty minutes, perhaps forty-five minutes. Mr. Rainbow's command performance with me would have lasted no more than ten minutes. The whole episode from go-to-whoa would have been less than an hour in duration. Sometimes, we think that our lives are small and insignificant. We wonder who cares about what we think or feel or say. We doubt our influence on each other. I have never forgotten either the young man with hydrocephaly in all his self-acceptance and Mr. Rainbow's praise for a job well done.

At this time, I was invited to attend a meeting at the Cornwall Street Deaf School in Annerley. It was a committee meeting. The details are hazy now. It was a bright summer day; we sat in a ramshackle room, long table, wooden chairs, piles of papers around the perimeter of the room, papers on the table too. I looked out the window several times, wanted to be outside. It was hard to follow what was being said. There was a lot of mumbling, rustling of papers. The other people sitting around the table looked old; they *were* old. They all wore suits, the women as well as the men.

Actually, not all of them were old. A younger man was present; he was deaf too. He was a cheerful, smiley man. He and I were the only deaf people on this committee that apparently represented the interests of deaf people. We had been invited onto this committee because we were deaf. I knew this was the reason when I received and accepted the invitation, but now that I was in this room, I felt prickly. Nothing I said was cutting through. The old men in their suits turned to me when I spoke, nodded thoughtfully, and resumed their discussion as if I had not spoken. The old women smiled encouragingly at me, but they did not intervene for me. They did not call out to those old men, "Hey! This young woman has something of substance to listen to." I felt the oppression of being dumb. Not dumb as in stupid; dumb as in being unable to speak with conviction. The cheerful, smiley man spoke a couple of times. Nothing he said cut through either.

I went to one more committee meeting and pulled the pin. I did not go back. More than this, I did not advocate in public again about what it means to be deaf for thirty years. Instead, I made a vow of sorts, not quite a vow of silence, more a vow of mutiny. I did not see the old committee men's behavior as entirely sexist, although there was the inevitable flavor of "elderly men pitted against young woman" tone to our interactions. Instead, I felt and saw and understood the experience very much as "hearing superiority" versus "deaf naiveté." I simmered about this for a while, not knowing how to ask advice from my friends. In the end, I opted for a militant sort of silence. I chose the path of doing as well as I could without talking about it, without drawing people's attention to my deafness. Just as my thoughts of God had been inchoate, so were my thoughts about how to make my mark. All I knew was this: talking about what a deaf person can do was not going to be enough. I would show what a deaf person can do, and I would show it with as few words as possible.

In the course of my professional life, I was sometimes asked whether my deafness affected my ability to do my work. I always said no. The short answer was easier than the long answer, which was, "It doesn't affect my capacity to work but it may affect the sort of work that I can do. However, with the right technology and suitable adaptations, perhaps I can tackle all sorts of work and handle any situation that arises. It also affects the way I work; I make sure I am well organized and as ahead of the game as possible." (This degree of preparation had its obvious advantages in that it put me in a good professional light, but it also bred an inflexibility into my work habits. I hated being surprised by an unexpected deadline or thrown a new task on short notice.) Saying no catapulted me into the jobs

I wanted, but it also held me back from asking for help. I may have taken my mother's philosophy of "Don't complain—act!" too much to heart, but having said no, I felt that I could not reasonably turn around and say, "Well, actually . . ." I did not ask for, nor expect, any allowances to be made for me, and when they were made, I was surprised and grateful.

Take the time when I arrived to my new job in England: On discovering I was deaf, my work colleagues reorganized all the office furniture—desks, computers, shelving, the whole shebang—so that I could see what they were all saying. They did this entirely on their own initiative and with English cheer. They were nonplussed that I had not asked for this consideration in the first place. "Oy! We can't have you sitting there with your back to us. How will you know when we're making fun of you?" Nick demanded. And then there was the time when the director-general of a government department observed my unusual silence in a board of management meeting. The long and narrow board room had been newly refurbished with recessed, low-voltage ceiling lights. She looked around the table where my colleagues sat with their faces cast in shadow and drew her conclusions. Not one to shilly-shally, she pulled me aside after the meeting and said, "I'll fix the lights. What else do you need?"

But fitting in had been a driving force in my professional life. I may have taken Robert Frost's the road less traveled on other matters, but I was uncomfortable about rocking the boat when it came to asserting my rights as a deaf woman in the workplace. My frustrations would simmer and then erupt as a burst of Delphic commentary, catching others by surprise. When a senior executive with a recidivist history of whispering, despite knowing that I could not hear him, once gave an address to my team and closed with the usual question, "Any comments?" I burned with resentment. "I haven't heard a single word you said." He nodded, murmured unwaveringly sotto voce, "Ah yes, you have a hearing problem, don't you?" I snapped, "No, you have a speech and courtesy problem." As if pulled by a puppet master's string, the gaze of all eyes in the room slanted down to inspect the grain and polish of the conference table. I leant back in my chair and fumed.

Even as I write about these isolated incidents, I struggle to find the right way to describe the relationship between my deafness and my professional life. I am not convinced there *is* one. My curriculum vitae reveals a busy career, filled with work as a social worker, researcher, policy advisor and writer, taking me to places across Australia and England and back again. My staff must have made adjustments, either to accommodate my needs or to orient themselves to the unusual spectacle of reporting to a senior manager who was deaf. I know that some of my colleagues thought I was intense or aloof before realizing that my deafness meant that I wasn't *ignoring* them; I just hadn't *heard* them; they had to get my attention before speaking with me. Sometimes, my workmates gathered anecdotes of mishaps to share at office Christmas parties; they were done in good humor, and actually, a few of the stories *were* funny . . . such as the time when I gave a presentation on disability to an audience of families and service providers in outback Queensland. A grazier sitting next to one of my colleagues said, "She speaks well for someone with a cleft palate, doesn't she?" My colleague realized the grazier had mistakenly attributed the cause of my speech impediment and sought to disabuse him by replying, "Actually, she's deaf." The grazier grimaced and shook his head in a display of dismay. "Oh dear God, a cleft palate *and* deaf. The poor girl." My colleague told me later, "Oh, what the hell. Let him feel sorry for you."

One feature of my work life stands out for me. I had never worked with another deaf public servant—let alone another deaf senior manager or executive—until I met James Strachan in England. This is a story worth telling in its entirety.

On a bleak January morning of low grey sky and sleet, a colleague and I caught an early train from Rochester in Kent to Charing Cross in London to go to a conference about reforms taking place at national and local government levels in Britain. It was headlined by politicians and bureaucrats, including David Blunkett, then the secretary of state for the Home Office, and James Strachan, then the chairman of the Audit Commission. David Blunkett was recognizably blind, as he was always accompanied by his guide dog. He was also a dull speaker, and so I was lulled into a slouch by watching his dog instead of attending to the drone of his voice directed to one side of the auditorium; his advisor had not positioned him squarely at the microphone. When James Strachan walked onto the stage, I hoped that he would be a livelier speaker, but I had no great expectations.

His voice startled me into sitting up straight. It had the slightly strangled speech-tones of a deaf person; he tended, like me, to "pop" some of his sounds especially the "p" and "m" sounds, those sounds that require compressing your lips. His face was expressive; he reminded me of my old Deaf School friends in the way he animated his words with a thrust of his hands and a tilt of his head. He used his whole body in a sway of communication. A stirring of compatriot recognition moved within me. James Strachan was deaf! The skin on my forearms goose-bumped and I had to fight the impulse to stand up and cheer, "Go James!" In that penny-dropping way, I could not recall witnessing any other deaf person in a position of such public prominence. I felt proud of him, as if I could claim some of his success. I looked around at the audience to gauge their reactions, and realized that I was not only enjoying what he was saying in such an authoritative and commanding manner—"For goodness sake, just get on with it!" he cried out—but I was also enjoying his achievement in having attained such a high profile, influential position in public life. I imagined that I understood the extent of his success. As I sat there in that crowded auditorium, alongside some of the most talented civil servants in the United Kingdom, I understood too the power of role models. I felt stirred in a way that I had not experienced before; watching James perform with such leadership, despite his evident profound deafness, made me want to strive for a similar challenge. I had turned my back on the senior executive life in the Queensland public service to come to England, and I wondered, that morning, about the wisdom of that decision. Or was I just caught up in the drama of James Strachan's appearance on the stage?

During the morning tea break, I scrutinized him through the filter of my deaf sensibilities. He spoke quickly and at length as if to fend off the threat of any more words going toward him, as if to deflect the possibility of having to struggle more than he cared for to understand what was being said. His expression was watchful, his eyes scanned the faces of his questioners, and he leant forward to attend to them all the more intently. His concentration was flattering: I could imagine people being willing to confide in him, trusting in his attentiveness.

I had not been looking for such a person, but when James Strachan appeared that day, I felt a relief that I did not fully understand. I wanted to speak with him urgently, to learn more about him, but I hesitated. I did not want to embarrass him or myself. I did not want him to think that I regarded him as being simply and elementally deaf. Equally and impossibly, I wanted him to recognize in me during that first moment of introduction as being a comrade-in-arms, a co-conspirator in the drama of deaf people taking up front-stage positions in the theater of the hearing world. I braced myself with courage and walked toward him, smiling as I did so. James turned toward me, his eyes ready for conversation, as I extended my hand of greeting and looked up at his lips.

I stammered. James Strachan came to the rescue by exclaiming, "You're an Australian!" and spoke confidently about the Australian National Audit Office's work. Eventually I blurted out why I really wanted to speak with him: "I'm deaf too!" He looked momentarily appalled. His unpreparedness for my claim took him off-guard, and he flushed deeply. I could see that he felt belittled, as if I was only interested in him as an object of curiosity and not because of his evident achievements and wit. I saw this because this is how I feel when people comment to me on my deafness, as if I must be wearing a billboard hanging around my neck with the words "Look at me! I'm deaf!" I rushed to fill the space that my gaffe had created, "I'm sorry to disturb you, but I really wanted to ask you if you would read an essay on deafness that I've written. I'd like to include you in it. Would that be okay? I would be very grateful." By now, I was sweating with the heat of my effrontery. James was agreeable to this and seemed bemused. "By all means, of course." I started to say something else—I wanted to acknowledge the awkwardness of being seen as a role model—but I shook my head to wave my words away and said, "No, I'll leave it." He laughed out loud at this,

"You are having trouble organizing your words. I can see that!" sparking in me a candle-flame of affection for him.

I finished my essay the very next day, reporting on my excitement on discovering James Strachan, and e-mailed it to him immediately. I hoped to hear from him soon; I promised myself not to harass him. "Give him time to digest it. Wait at least six weeks before following it up," but I didn't have to hold myself to this promise because he texted me on my mobile just two weeks later, on Saint Valentine's Day, while I was walking with friends in the Lakes District. He wrote of being moved by my essay, as was his partner, Tessa; it resonated for him; our experiences were so very similar; would I join him for lunch at Westminster soon? I was jubilant and wrote in my diary that night, "Is this a turning point?" I pinned my hopes for something—but what?—on this chance meeting with James Strachan.

James also e-mailed me with a transcript of a BBC radio interview he had done the previous year. The typed transcript was headlined "No Triumph, No Tragedy" and opened with the interviewer's words, "James Strachan's career suggests a man in a hurry. Cambridge at 16, youngest managing director of Merrill Lynch, the investment bank, at 32, then gave that all up to pursue one of his great loves—photography, and became a photojournalist. Then another complete change to become only the second deaf chief executive of the RNID, the Royal National Institute for Deaf People. . . . But earlier this year he moved on again—still the RNID's chairman, he's also now chairman of the Audit Commission. . . . Partially deaf as a child, he's now profoundly deaf and in face-to-face interviews, like this one, he lip reads." I read on. He was right; we did have experiences in common. He chose to lipread rather than sign "because that's how I was brought up"; he attributed his success to "a combination of determination, luck and the people around us"; he had "a very determined mother who was very keen to make sure that this [deafness] impacted me as little as possible"; and "the deafness just made me very hardworking, some would now say a workaholic." While he was diplomatic in his responses to the interviewer's questions about British Sign Language and whether deafness is a hearing loss problem or a culture with its own language and customs, he was adamant that "common sense needs to intervene" in debates about the rights of deaf children, especially if they can benefit significantly from a hearing aid or other technology such as cochlear implants. I nodded as I read the transcript of his words, scribbling notes in the margins, "just like me" and "yes." He hammered the interviewer's challenge that he could be accused of trying to hide his deafness:

> I don't think it's a question of hiding it as much as you can. I mean frankly my deafness impacts every millisecond of my life, except perhaps when I'm fast asleep at night blissfully unaware of what's going on around me. And it has influenced my life obviously very, very significantly. So to suggest one's hiding it is not the right word, it's a question of everybody has a range of strengths and weaknesses and it's a question of what you actually want to draw attention to.

I caught the catch-22 that James lived with: the extent of his success evidently raised doubts in other people's minds about him. Just exactly how deaf was he? Why doesn't he *act deaf*?

Early the following month, I met James at Shepherds, a restaurant near the Houses of Parliament. My pulse racing, I arrived a little early. He arrived a little late. My early arrival gave me time to take in the pencil portrait of Michael Caine, the actor, featured at the bottom of the parchment-like menu in homage to his status as a part-owner of the restaurant. James's late arrival gave him cause to press both my hands in a smiling greeting. I flushed pinkly as I felt the candlelight of affection for him reignite.

James took charge of the conversation, quizzing me about my life but offering only small glimpses into his own life. I learnt that his partner, Tessa, was a government minister and that he was a keen tennis player. He marveled, "You're the second Australian woman I've met in as many weeks. You might know her?" I laughed, "There are twenty million Australians, and it's a big country." James's questioning of my life was so dogged that it seemed as if he was interviewing me. He was boyishly enthusiastic, exclaiming several times, "Yes! That's right! I know what you mean!"

Eventually, he looked at his watch; he had a three o'clock judicial review appointment and had to rush off. We chatted a while longer on the footpath outside the restaurant, apparently reluctant to take our leave of each other. Finally, as raindrops began to sprinkle upon us, James pushed open his umbrella and we kissed each other thrice on the cheeks, French style.

At the office, the colleague who had accompanied me to that conference challenged me, "You haven't fallen in love with him, have you?" He took to teasing me at every opportunity, "How's your new boyfriend?" I affected an air of pained tolerance, but secretly, I did have a crush on James. The fact that James was deaf was deeply attractive to me; not only was he smart and funny, but he was *deaf*! He seemed to be deaf in the same way as I was deaf: he accepted his deafness without sentiment—neither romantic nor resentful—and took on the challenge of being fully immersed in the hearing world. Not only that, he was a high professional achiever just as I have strived to be professionally achieving (although I was, admittedly, not in his league). I had never dated a deaf man. I had had the occasional meal with a childhood deaf friend—Matthew, the one who showed off his strength to me as a four-year-old boy by picking up my chair and who now visited me each year around Christmastime—but my affection for him remained filial. In contrast, my lunch with James set my imagination alight. Honestly, I was suffused with joy. I had talked happily and unguardedly with James in a way that was unusual for me. I had told my stories to him as performance, freeing my hands into gestures arcing through the air, and softening my face into the shapes of frowns, arched eyebrows, grimaces and smiles to illustrate what I was saying.

I was flattered, too, by James's belief in my writing. "You must persevere and shape the essay into a book one day," he had said. He asked me to think about working with the Royal National Institute for the Deaf and, in a later e-mail, commissioned me to write an article for their journal. I wrote about the sounds of England. I remembered how, at first, I was self-conscious about the paddock-wide sound of my Australian voice in contrast to the channeled English vowels of restraint. My voice seemed to clatter and skid all over the place. I had been so anxious about speaking that my jaw was sore with tension. I also had to tackle the regional variations in dialects which are much greater than in Australia; a variety of accents crossed my sound field every day, forcing me to constantly recalibrate the way I read speech. I encountered new sounds I could not hear: when a colleague invited me to walk through the woods of Canterbury one spring evening to listen to the nightingales sing, I was wry. "It's a lovely invitation, but all I would hear is the quiet of the night."

James's advocacy as the chair of the Royal National Institute for the Deaf provoked me into thinking less about my relationship with my own deafness and more about my contribution to the public understanding of other deaf people's lives. And yet, for all my enthusiasm for James, and despite writing in my diary, "End the essay on a note of continuing discovery," I had balked then at exploring my deafness further. I had shied away from the threshold that I had imagined separated my hearing-world persona from a consuming vortex of deaf identity.

Back in Brisbane, I tracked down George, my first work supervisor from all those years ago. I wanted to find out why he had taken a chance on me to give me my first job and then arranged for a special telephone adaptor with a volume control so that I could conduct conversations on the office telephone. As we sat across from each other in a city coffee shop, I asked my question. I waited for him to launch into a spiel about affirmative action and fairness. He looked down into his cup of coffee, laughed in a nervous hiccoughing way, and said, "It didn't hurt that you were good-looking."

I was amused by this and enjoyed repeating George's claim to my friends, but I was also stymied by it. It didn't ring true. It had the hallmark of skirting around the issue, of being evasive. Was he afraid of treading where angels fear to go? It's possible. After all, I *had* been angry, years earlier, to learn that I had been recruited as a social worker at a center for children with a disability, not because of my qualifications and expertise, but because of my deafness. Even though the children were not deaf—they had cerebral palsy—my deafness apparently conferred me with the wisdom to establish a special rapport with them and with their parents. My manager at that center was sprightly and unapologetic about her reason for recruiting me. I had felt diminished.

George's claim, good-humored though it was, resurrected that memory of diminishment. It also reminded me of my resolve in the early days of my professional life. It didn't matter, in the end, why people employed me; what mattered was that I proved my worth.

12

Talking about Deafness

I was invited onto a national radio show, *Richard Fidler's Conversation Hour*, to talk about my experiences as a deaf woman. It is customary to confess to nerves when confronted with the prospect of speaking in public, but any sign of nerves that I may have had—the dry palate, the beads of perspiration caught in the groove of my top lip, the jigging left foot—gave way to a greater emotion about thirty seconds into the interview: zeal. The interviewer was friendly and well prepared; a script rested on his lap. I leant forward to catch his questions and cradled them with care to make sure that I gave them my very best attention and my most honest answers. While I was used to fending the occasional question here and there about my deafness, I was a novice in fielding such a cascade of them in public, over a thirty-minute period. I met the patter of questions with mounting energy and accelerating emotion, bearing witness to the strength of my attachment to my deafness.

Listeners would have heard my voice quaver as I spoke of my mother's observations that I was a watchful child, that deafness was once a taboo subject, that I had to be taught there was such a thing as sound before I could be taught how to interpret it and to find meaning in sound, that I went to great lengths to recreate silence because I found it peaceful, that

I believed that the purpose of communication lies in our ability to forge relationships, and that whether we speak with our voices or with the grammar of our hands accented by the expressions on our faces and the sway of our bodies, *this* is the most important thing, to relate, and that I regarded my own deafness as just a part of life, no more, no less. I was vehement in response to a question about the advantages of hearing, and let fall a tumble of words.

> Of course it's good to hear. It's a simple fact of life that most of the world is hearing. . . . It's also a simple unadorned fact of life that we need to engage with each other as people, friends, lovers. . . . Given that the dominant communication is speech, of course it's good to be able to hear and participate in that. However, if you are so deaf that you cannot communicate by speech, then you learn other ways of communication. . . . For me the question is not, is it good to hear or not to hear? The question revolves around, what does it take to help us communicate with each other?

I left the recording studio that warm August afternoon pumped with the adrenaline rush that comes with the relief of confession. I had told *my* story of deafness, put it out there in public in contest with that odd mixture of sad-sack and triumphalist stories of deafness, and felt flushed with exposure.

The interview was played on air the next day and was to be repeated the following year in conjunction with a planned interview with Graeme Clark, the inventor of the cochlear implant. I was not sure what I had started or where I was going with this public foray. I was unsure of my motivation for agreeing to this interview. I worried about being seen as a role model, even while understanding that I wanted to reach out to those young parents coming to terms with their children's deafness. I also hoped to flush out other deaf people and other deaf stories.

It was not the first time I had been interviewed about my deafness. When I was eleven years old, I took part in a television documentary. I was attending All Hallows by then, but the interview took place in one of the classrooms at the Oral Deaf Preschool at Yeronga; large lamps were set up in the room, shining a hot glare in my direction and throwing the corners of the room into darkness. I had recently had a tooth extracted from the back of my mouth and showed off the gap to the interviewer—and to the viewing audience—by opening my mouth like a wide-mouthed frog. Several years later at my father's urging, I submitted myself to more newspaper interviews and photographs when I graduated from university with my first degree. I was mildly embarrassed by this and let myself be teased by my friends for "taking up modeling." I bought into my father's belief that the newspaper articles about my graduation might be helpful for parents of deaf children, but I felt uncomfortable about the way my deafness was pulled out of a hat from time to time to make a specific point but was then pushed down into the background for the rest of the time to make a different point.

After listening to the recording of my interview on the radio the next day in the comfort of my home, I felt drained and weepy. I received several congratulatory e-mails from friends and acquaintances, including old school friends whom I had not seen since our final exams. An e-mail also arrived from the sister of a deaf veterinary scientist, George, who had attended the Deaf School a few years ahead of me; I remembered his name—my mother had spoken of his brilliance—and my skin tingled as I read the pride in her words about her brother's achievements, including his role as a consultant to the World Health Organization. Filled with that nervous anticipatory excitement of a first date, I wrote back to her, which in turn sparked a series of reminiscing, funny e-mails with George for several weeks. My own sister sent me a text message giving me the thumbs up; she thought the interview was very good. Still, I felt hollow-hearted. I wondered why. I was teary on hearing myself recount my distress on realizing that I had been the source of pain and panic for my parents simply because I was deaf, a characteristic over which I had no control. I thought that I could compare deafness with autism, which I considered to be a devastating disability. At least parents can relate to their deaf child, I thought. Much later on, I learnt from my mother that this, in fact, was her very fear:

that she would not be able to communicate with me, her youngest daughter; that I would not be able to talk with her. She told of seeing deaf people in the shopping center, signing and "drawing attention to themselves." She reveled in the fact that I could talk to her, that she could talk to me.

After listening to the radio interview, I rang my mother, but she didn't answer the phone. When I tried again a couple of hours later, she wore her matter-of-fact tone of voice.

"I've just been down the road to visit Enid," she said. "It was a very nice interview. I told Enid about it."

"But how did I sound? Did I sound all right? What was my voice like?"

"I thought you spoke very well. Your voice was very clear." She paused. At my end of the telephone line, several suburbs away, I could sense my mother choosing her next words. "Everything you said was clear and appropriate."

I didn't press her for more. It was enough, for the time being, that I had sounded clear and appropriate.

I pushed on. By now, my befuddled curiosity about my relationship with my deafness had swelled to a desire to leave the enclosed space of the hearing world and to find my way into the deaf community. I wanted to test my deaf credentials as it were. My Melbourne friend, Michael, told me about an upcoming national conference for the deaf; he emboldened me to submit a paper for presentation at the conference. Sandi e-mailed me: she was heading off to this conference as well; we promised to meet up there, and I felt as though I was preparing for another first date. I had picked up a new work project with the Education Department following my protracted illness of several weeks earlier but my mind moved restlessly away from work, away even from my family, friends, and routines. Preoccupied by what I would say at the conference and how I would fit into the deaf community, I moved through my days in a fuguelike state.

I was surprised by the size of the conference. Several hundred people milled around in the foyer and spilled into the convention rooms. Their pitching voices, gesturing hands, lively faces and tilting, swaying bodies appeared before me like the curtain rise of a theatrical event. It was exciting. *I* was excited. I turned to a woman standing next to me, tapped her gently on the arm to catch her eyes. "Excuse me, do you know where the films are being shown?" And in that splinter of time waiting for her reply, I saw that I was looking at Sandra. I had not seen her since I was a child of six years old and only God knows how, perhaps it was her red hair, but I just knew it was her. I bent down to peer at her name card for confirmation but her eyes widened in the same second of recognition and her mouth opened in a laugh of joy: "Donna! You are so beautiful! Oh!" We hugged as if we would never let each other go again. We didn't yet know much about the surface details of each other's lives, but our intuition of an underground life, of subterranean emotions that have to be mined deeply before being exposed and shared, bound us in that moment. Over the two days of the conference, Sandra and I listened to each other; in our listening, we heard the other's courage, and understood at last that courage shone within both of us.

I found Michael too. We signaled our way to each other with the help of our mobile telephones, smiling as we bumped together upon our arrival at the same spot. Several people jostled for Michael's attention, thumped him on an arm or cried out in greetings of delight; he was evidently something of a celebrity in this world. And through Michael, I reunited with Bridget, my former flatmate from university days, who carried herself now with a still poise, as if she was listening out for a long-ago musical note that hung in the air there, just beyond her reach, like the last falling autumn leaf. Billed as the keynote speaker, Bridget was highly respected, and she held both the attention and the affection of her audience; they nodded often and waved-clapped at regular intervals during her presentation. Her topic was the place of deaf people in colonial Australia and their access (or lack of it) to justice, education, and employment. I liked her detective approach to understanding deaf lives by sifting through the sands of mainstream history. I also felt prickles of envy, admiration, and regret; Bridget had given so much of herself to improving the understanding of deaf people's lives. I judged myself: shouldn't I have done this myself, so much earlier? I brooded as her PowerPoint slides flickered across the screen. I was learning that courage lay within me, but I saw my cowardice too. I felt that I should have tried harder to bridge my two worlds; I should not have relied so heavily on Matthew, my annual visitor from my deaf childhood, to be the message-bearer from my deaf world. Could I now make up for lost time? And how?

My conference paper received a mixed reception. It was about stories of deafness by hearing writers. I told the audience about T. C. Boyle's energetic novel *Talk Talk*—the title is a translation of "conversation" from sign into English; "Talk talk. That was what happened when the deaf got together . . . they talked a lot, talked all the time." This fast-paced novel features a deaf heroine, Dana, and the drama that unfolds when she discovers that she is the victim of credit-card identity theft. Dana drives across North America with her boyfriend, Bridger, in pursuit of the thief. Throughout this adventure, we learn about Dana's deaf-life, including her attempt to write a book about the Wild Child of Aveyron, found at the age of eleven or twelve living ferally in Napoleonic France and, as Dana explains to Bridger, "Her throat constricting, . . . 'he never did learn to speak'" despite the efforts of a teacher, Itard. Through Dana's eyes, we also learn about the impact of deafness on relationships; deaf politics, including the politics of sign language versus oral speech; hearing technology such as cochlear implants; and the implications of these for Dana's sense of self.

Boyle's treatment of all this material is more nuanced than this list might suggest. He catches the paradox of the fragility of Dana's integration of her deaf-self into her generally exuberant personality. Dana's boyfriend, Bridger, reveals more in his reminiscences about the first time he met her in a dance club and in his continuing curiosity, sometimes clumsily expressed, about her deafness. When Dana recounts the joy of a deaf couple upon learning that their baby was deaf—"'Thank God,' they said, 'she's one of us'"—Bridger asks, "And what do you mean by that?" Their conversation becomes strained with Bridger's confusion and Dana's hurt:

> "But that isn't you," he said, fumbling around the issue. "I mean, you're not like that."

"I don't understand."

"You're not—I mean, you weren't born like that. Right?"

She'd looked as if she was going to cry, but now she forced a smile.

"Born like what?"

"Deaf . . ."

At the age of four and a half she'd been stricken with spinal meningitis . . . [and] her aural nerves had been irreparably damaged . . . "Yes," she told him, reaching to bury her hand in the bag of potato chips as if to hide it from him, as if she were afraid of what it might say otherwise, "that's not me."

Bridger's assertion "You're not like that," carries the hearing person's doubt of prejudice coupled with their superior sense of self when confronted with deafness. The question of whether Dana was born deaf or acquired it through illness is irrelevant to her. She is deaf. Her hearing loss was not just a single physiological, auditory incident. It continued to shape her sense of self in the wake of people's responses to her deaf characteristics: "Her atonal voice, the non sequiturs, the fluidity of her face when she spoke, as if every muscle under the skin were a separate organ of communication." Boyle's empathy for Dana was so compelling that I caught myself learning from Dana's efforts to integrate her deaf-self into her hearing-world life.

In my conference paper, I contrasted Boyle's novel with Frances Itani's depressing novel, *Deafening*. This could be read simply as a love story about a young deaf woman, Grania, and her hearing husband, Jim. However, Itani has accomplished much more than this. Her novel is an extended tutorial about deafness based on her memories of her deaf grandmother, illustrating the historical, social, and cultural context of deaf people's lives in Canada during the early 1900s and the Great War. This was a time when educational debates about signing versus oralism were intense and bitter, and Itani portrays deafness as a burdensome thing, not only for the deaf person but also for families and society in general.

Itani's evocation of a deaf life is obsessively melancholic, but her observations of the things that make life different for a deaf person are authentic.

She establishes her authority quickly in the novel. In just two short pages, Itani tells the story of Grania's hearing loss through a childhood illness (scarlet fever); the parental grief and sibling pragmatism to Grania's deafness; the dilemmas of speech, lipreading, and signing—"Tress and Grania have already begun to make up their own language, with their hands"; schooling; social reactions—"People will think she's stupid"; the marital stress experienced by Grania's parents; the power of the spoken word—"If you can say your name, you can tell the world who you are"; and the importance of inclusion—"Include her in everything." Itani also describes the emotion of lip movements when they are read by a deaf person—"Bernard's lips smile when he says the end of her name"; "When Tress calls her Graw, her jaw drops"; and "Mother's lips make a straight line. She does not smile or laugh."

Grania's deafness is seen as a shadow that falls across her entire life. Even her prospects for marriage are seen to be diminished. Cora, one of the characters in the novel, asks, "Who will marry that pitiful child when she grows up? . . . If they don't find someone deaf and dumb, she'll end up living with her mother the rest of her days." (My own fear about my solitariness gorged forth when I read this.) When Grania meets and marries a hearing man, Jim, the reader is led to understand that he is a good man. He is, after all, a doctor who heals people.

Itani not only designs a fictionalized family account dominated by Grania's deafness, but she also portrays Grania's own interior world as one that is cannibalized by her lifelong contemplation of her deafness. Even when Grania finally stands up for herself against Cora's bullying, she regards her own anger through the lens of her deafness, "The raised voice of the deaf, this is what it sounds like when we don't keep it close." Grania's self-absorption about her deafness is so persistent that it inevitably jars. It also has the effect of infantilizing Grania by not granting her the maturity to look outside of herself and into the concerns of others. In fact, Itani reinforces Grania's childlike status throughout the entire novel by showing Grania conjuring up characters from her childhood storybooks in times of stress, with the character of Dulcie making frequent appearances. Itani's portrayal of Grania in deaf adulthood as forever caught in the world of girlhood stories mirrors the way deaf people are diminished in real life.

The notion of deafness as a heavy weight set alight within me a long, slow burning fuse of sullen resentment that persisted throughout my reading of it. I did not want *this* to be the story of deafness that is told today. My suspicion about the potential of Itani's novel to cast a cloak of misunderstanding about the possibilities of contemporary deaf lives was fueled when one of my closest friends confided, "I understand what your life is like now." I was appalled. "You've got to be kidding!"

That afternoon at the conference, I wanted to share my lessons from these novels with the audience and to unburden my urgency for deaf people to tell our own stories—written, spoken, or signed—of our deaf lives. I wanted to abolish the notion that our lives swung or fell on the pivot of our deafness. I wanted to lay out our deafness within the texture of our dreams and our hopes and our achievements, and our failings too. But my words only struck home here and there; unlike Bridget and Michael, I was too much of an unknown to this audience. I looked at the people sitting before me, saw three or four interested faces—their eyes were directed toward either me or the Auslan interpreter standing next to me—but I also saw that most of the people were distracted. Some flicked desultorily through their conference papers; others conducted signed conversations across the rows of chairs; still others had their eyes closed. The audience was straining for the conference to end. I was the second-to-last speaker on the program, and, wilting before their boredom, I hurried my words along, confused the interpreter, and thus, in turn, confused the already restless audience.

It may have been because the conference was heavily slanted to the Auslan signing community, but oralism seemed to be accepted only with enforced gentility, a feigned tolerance. In fact, one of the conference speakers claimed that "oral deaf people live in a suspended state . . . in denial of their deafness." My chest tightened. This was maddening. I rejected the judgments that swung on the axis of claim and counterclaim in which oral deaf people are either regarded as "success stories" by the hearing world or as "deniers" by the Deaf community.

I came away from the conference disappointed. I could not put my finger on the source of my disappointment at the time. Certainly the lack of
interest in my paper piqued my vanity, but my discontent ran deeper than
that. I had run into a briar bush when I had been hoping to be gathered
into the folds of a welcoming community. When I thought about this conference again sometime later, I saw that I had not yet learned how to say
what I wanted to say or how to ask the questions I wanted to ask; I was
overly sensitive about the risk of hurting people. I also recognized that as
an outsider to this particular community, I had to do more to gain their
attention and trust. Presenting just one conference paper was, of course,
not going to cut any ice. And finally, I realized something else. I was too
conscious about the gifts of speech and language that I had been given,
and I was not about to use those gifts as missiles directed toward either
camp, deaf or hearing. Virtuous though this ambition might have been, I
suspected that my efforts at diplomacy may have been viewed either with
distrust or skepticism by the people I was trying to reach out to.

13

Falling for His Line

Damian rang. Caught me off guard. We chatted. I tried to give off an air of heartiness. He backed out of the conversation with the promise to call me again soon, very soon, to make a time for us to get together for a cup of coffee. Being a literal-minded sort of a woman, I took him at his word. I waited for his call.

14

Will I Still Be Deaf When I Grow Up?

"Thank you for saying my name!" my friend Sharon exclaimed.

I had sent Sharon, my best friend at the deaf school—the one with the shy smile and hair tied back into a ponytail—a copy of my published essay, "I Hear with My Eyes." It included my reminiscences about our childhood friendship, a time when we were so close that people mistook us for twins. In my packet of photos from that time, I treasured one black-and-white photo in particular; worn around the edges from frequent handling, it showed Sharon and me at a school fete. We had the chubby-cheeked appearance of five-year-olds, looking pleased with ourselves as we tore wrapping paper from the parcels on our laps. In another photo, possibly snapped on the same day, Sharon and I were dressed as fairies wearing wings of voile stretched across wire frames, wands with flying ribbons and paper star-embossed crowns on our heads.

Sharon had already written a note of thanks to me, but now she reached out to hug me, her cheeks pinking and her eyelashes catching the first fall of tears from her bluer-than-blue, almond-shaped eyes. She had not even put her purse down yet. We were standing in my kitchen, admiring each other and talking across each other, falling over our words to conjure up old memories and new stories. She looked terrific. She wore a black and cream outfit with a matching rope of beads around her neck. Her hair was streaked with golden-blonde highlights, showing off her flawless skin, and her eyebrows were perfectly shaped, arched like a 1950s Hollywood star. "I cried and cried when I read your essay," she wept. "It brought everything back. I remembered everything as it was. What it was like back then. What we were like." Her tears prickled my own always-latent tears into life as I stood there smiling foolishly at her. I was transfixed by her choice of words. It seemed to me that Sharon's excitement went beyond the frisson of seeing her name in print. It sounded like the deep relief of being recognized. I saw that I had breathed life into *her* story by writing her name not just once in that essay of mine but three times; and more than this, she had not regarded the saying of her name thrice over as a betrayal of her privacy but as an affirmation of her own place in history, even if it was just in the personal history of a long-ago friend.

We had first renewed our childhood friendship during my university years and her early working years; faded holiday snapshots showed us sitting in our bikinis on Balmoral Beach, and dressed in Victorian-period costumes, complete with bonnets, during a visit to the historic Rocks District of Sydney. We confided in each other about our romantic misadventures. Sharon had ended a brief courtship with one of my work colleagues, even though he shaved off his beard to show his commitment to her. We had each dated the same man a few times, a smooth-talking doctor with a sports car who may or may not have had a fetish for deaf women. I had gone to her wedding and watched her exchange vows with a good man (not the doctor). Our Christmas cards found their way to each other through all our changes of address across all the years and marked out the differences in our lives—she with her two children, husband, and stability; me with my professional life, chasing dreams of romantic love. Our most recent conversation had taken place at Lake Currimundi, where I was holidaying with other friends. Sharon lived nearby. We had walked along the beach that day, the sea wind whipping our hair across our faces and lashing the sand on our legs, and chatted happily about this and that.

Time passed. All fourteen years of it. For no particular reason but for every reason in the world, we had not seen each other since. She could not use the phone; I had not made the time either to call her husband or to discover her e-mail address; she was busy with her children and homemaking, I buried myself in work and wondered how people ever found the time to work and manage a family life at the same time; she lived by the beach and I lived in the inner city, we were only a short car trip apart but . . . no more buts. It was never too late or too hard to reach across time's divides. I rang Tess, Sharon's mother, who greeted me as if I was a regular caller, unfazed by the gap of fourteen years that had fallen between us. Tess had advised me a long time ago to "be careful not to fall too low in your spirits. It's too hard to climb back to the top again." It was good wisdom. I always heard it whenever I tottered on the edge of melancholy. She gave me Sharon's new address and telephone number. I rang Sharon's husband. We set up a lunch date at my home for the next month. It was as easy as that.

Now, we had much to catch up on and settled into a rhythm of newsgiving over our lunch as the afternoon lengthened into its mellow tones. Sharon talked with the usual mixture of a mother's joy and exasperation about her now adult children, and I updated her on the news of my eight nieces and nephews. This transformation of children into adults induced in us a marvel at the passage of time. We took an inventory of our childhood classmates, sharing the little that we knew, filling in the gaps where we could, and tried to avoid making up the rest. Some names conjured up their personalities, whole, bright, and vivid as ever: Matthew, Jennifer, Kay, Kenneth, Wayne, Carmel. "Matthew's carpentry business is going well," I said. "Carmel's eldest daughter is married to that A grade footballer," Sharon said. "Which one?" "I can't remember his name!" Other names propelled the faces of children to the foreground of my mind's eye, but I could not imagine them as they were now; it had been too long since my last sight of them: Norman, Margaret, Narelle, John, and the "other Donna," the one with curly hair. And some names had dropped out of our memory banks altogether: I could not remember Danny; Sharon could not remember Sandra. I told Sharon of my efforts to learn Auslan from Jennifer. She made a face. "Oh, that must be hard." She could make a few signs, the more obvious and easy ones, the universal gestures that we all know; we played them out to each other over our glasses of wine—"I love you," eating, having a cup of tea, buttering a slice of bread. But like me, she lived her life entirely in the oral, hearing world.

We laughed at my story about my nephew who had wanted to be deaf as a little boy, but Sharon bettered it with her own remembrance of childhood make-believe. She had had two little friends who lived in the house opposite her home. She said, "The three of us would play in the street together. I had my metal-box hearing aid tucked into a harness outside my dress." I could see in my mind's eye how the pink cord would have looped from it to her ear. "And my two friends had *their* hearing aids," Sharon broke into giggles. "They had matchboxes sticky-taped to their dresses, and their mother had twisted cotton thread around the matchboxes so that it was tied up to a wad of cotton wool jammed into their ears!" We both erupted into hee-hawing laughter at this, gulping our wine in hysteria. I loved the delicious harmony implicit in this image; I still smile each time I think about those three little girls playing in the street, all with their hearing aids, one real and two as real as their imaginations allowed them.

But one person's harmony is another person's crown of thorns. I mentioned that I had bumped into one of our childhood classmates, Kenneth, at a party several months earlier. I repeated his words to me, "You must write about us. Tell our stories. . . . You know about the Stolen Generations? Well, we are the Forgotten Generation." Sharon looked thoughtful. "It's a good thing to do, to write about us. People are interested. They want to know about deafness." She cautioned me. "Not everyone likes being deaf. I know some deaf people who ask, 'Why me?'" Sharon's brother was deaf, and she thought that deaf boys' experiences were different from deaf girls, that they were more likely to be bullied or hassled than girls. Her caution pulled me up short in a way that no hearing person's questions could ever do. I had been so intent for so long—in fact, almost lifelong—on defending my position as a person happy and content in her deafness that I had not only closed my heart to those people who find their deafness a source of pain and unhappiness, but I had also been relentless in my own denials.

An almost lifelong series of denials. All those small and big denials of embarrassment, hiding, retreating, coping, and laughing to cover up my hurts . . . pushing all those incidents down, down, and further down within me, out of sight, out of mind, out of reach.

One such incident kept surfacing as a story to be told and retold, not by me but by those who were present at the time. It happened several years earlier, just before my fortieth birthday, when I went with my swimming-club friends one weekend to Mooloolaba to take part in an interclub ocean swim. I am not a natural sportswoman: no eye-hand coordination for golf, tennis, or squash; no endurance for running; too squeamish for any of the contact sports; and no sense of spatial strategy for games such as netball and basketball. I can walk and I can swim. That's it. To swim 1,500 meters in the ocean felt like a victory. It *was* a victory. The prize was in doing it and I expected nothing more. A photograph taken of a group of us that day, wearing our swimsuits, shows me standing in the middle of the group, swim cap in hand, looking fit and happy.

That evening, everyone crowded into a holiday apartment overlooking the ocean to celebrate in a mess of wine, beer, and clowning around, but my elation had subsided. I strained to look enthusiastic. My hearing aid had died on me. A droplet of water had found its way from my wet hair into the microphone circuitry of my behind-the-ear aid (a CSI-like image comes to mind here). I only wore one hearing aid at the time and so did not have a spare. An accident like this had not happened to me before. Ever. I had once fallen (or was I pushed?) into a swimming pool when I was a child, prompting an urgent visit to the Acoustics Laboratory for a replacement hearing aid so that our family holiday to Sydney could proceed the next day. Aside from that, in all the holidays in all the beaches across all the countries in the world that I had ever visited, I had never had any such accidents with a droplet of water. I was angry too because the hearing aid was new. My old metal box hearing aid, hugged close to my body, would not have reacted so wimpishly. My swimming friends saw my tension; they were sympathetic. Jane reached for my hands, held them in her hands. Her smile was bright. "Stay! You'll be fine!" Wal and John called out, "You'll be okay!" Their exclamations were full of friendship. Persuaded, I stayed.

The unbelievable happened. A power blackout. A storm fierce with whipping winds, sheeting rain, and lightning strikes had brought down the power lines. The apartment snapped into coal-black. Not even a moon-light's glow threaded its way into the darkness. I felt movement, felt the pulse of wordless yells, and was nauseous with terror. Tight chest. Con-stricted throat. Asthmatically breathless. Wanted to run, run, and keep running from that place of blinding darkness and unreadable noise.

Cigarette lighters flickered; matches were struck and dropped, presum-ably in an exhalation of torched fingertips. MaryJane found her way to me in the darkness and, putting her face directly in front of me, clasped my shoulders, "Are you all right?" I shook my head. She wrapped an arm around my shoulders, either in sympathy or to brace me with much needed courage, or both. She repeated everyone's earlier belief in me, "You'll be all right. We'll look after you." She had more belief in me than I did. I could not bear it; could not bear to be in this room of noise without knowing what was going on. I wasn't frightened of what might physically happen to me, but I was fear-filled all the same. MaryJane's kindness unsettled me instead of soothing me. I did not understand why at the time. I did not allow myself to think about it. All I knew was that I had to escape from my panic and the only way to do that was to escape from this apart-ment of blinding noise. I would have endured the roped-neck tension of driving down the Bruce Highway in the pounding rain, the windshield wipers flailing against the waterfall, to reach the shelter of my home, but my swimming friends—worried about my safety on the wet highway—held me back, released me the next morning: the sky was clear, the sun shone once more. I was limp with relief when I finally turned my car into the driveway of my home, where I locked both the front and back doors against the world, slid down to the floor, and slumped into the comfort of my own silence.

While writing about this incident, which was intended to demonstrate the extent of my panic when faced with the failure of my hearing aids, I glimpsed another reason for my terror. My reaction to the swiftness of the black-falling darkness butting up against a vacuum of incomprehensible sound had anthropological antecedents. It was simply the primeval flight response to the threat of the unknown. But something else happened to me in that storm: a mask had been torn down, the mask of self-assurance, of being competently deaf in a hearing world. I had not even known I was wearing such a mask until the drop of water in my hearing aid, the black-fall, and MaryJane's kindness reflected back to me, mirrorlike, the public face of my vulnerability.

Apparently, a question commonly asked by little deaf children born into hearing families is "When I grow up, will I still be deaf?" They have so little experience of deaf adults in their lives that they wonder if deafness is something they will grow out of, stop being. I do not recall ever asking this question, but over the years, I must have learned the answer in a different way: I must have learned that it's possible, perhaps desirable, to relinquish your deaf-self even while retaining your deafness. So the task I took from my terror at the beach that night was to strive to be more competent and more vigilant against the threat of public displays of my deaf-self/hearing-persona clashes. I did not see it as a golden opportunity to relax my guard, to loosen the mask, or even to set it aside altogether. I did not consider the possibility of a free fall into trust. Trust in myself, in the adaptability of my deaf-self, coiled so tightly within. Or trust in my friends. A close friend from my university days wrote to me when I sent her an early draft of this chapter:

> When I reflected on what you had written, I felt an overwhelming disconnect because, I realized, you had clearly identified yourself as deaf, and I have never thought of you as deaf. . . . Anyway, on reading the words about your terror in the blackout, I was jolted by the realization that in all the years we have known one another, in the many turns of our friendship, I may have missed the very essence of who you are. . . . But I was also sad that you obviously worked so hard to put yourself into another skin—something more mainstream and acceptable. And that as a friend I did not question that you might want otherwise.

Even so, I was slow to grasp how my university friend's perception of me was now enriched and that this might, in turn, enrich our friendship.

Sharon and I promised to stay in touch. She said, "We must not lose each other again for so long." I hugged her tight in agreement and stepped back to watch her settle into her car and drive down the road and off around the corner. Even when her car was out of sight, I stayed on the footpath, reluctant to break the thread between us.

I rang my mother to tell her about my lunch with Sharon. When I said, "Sharon's voice is lovely," my mother's response was quick. "You've got a lovely voice too. That's because you both only mix with hearing people."

PART THREE

15

Shattered

My sleep grew frantic, billowing with dreams that tossed me back onto the morning shore, feeling ragged and bewildered. Confrontations with belligerent hearing people. Reunions with my childhood deaf friends. Journeys by buses and trains that never took me to where I was seeking to arrive. Lost with a burden of suitcases in English villages and scattered Australian suburbs. I often woke drenched in perspiration, and I wondered what was happening to me.

A few weeks before Christmas, Damian invited me to meet him for coffee at an inner-city bookshop-cafe. It had been some months since we had seen each other, and I was excited by his invitation. Damian's pleasure on the day was evident too. I looked up from flicking through the pages of a book in time to see his face light up when he saw me; it was as if a switch had been thrown. He sprinted through the bookshop's aisles and, on reaching me, clasped my arms and beamed down at me. We found a table and ordered our coffees, and he chatted about his work and his children. Everything was going well for him, he said. I saw that he was happy to see me, to be with me. Our conversation ebbed and flowed in the usual way of such conversations between a man and a woman caught up in the dance of anxiety and uncertain feelings. We laughed; we spoke seriously; we swapped stories and gossip; we even dared to reveal some of our worries.

When Damian asked me how my "deaf project" was coming along, I mentioned two memoirs I had just read, both written by Frances Warfield, an American journalist. The first was *Cotton in My Ears*, published in 1948, and the second was *Keep Listening*, published in 1957. The memoirs bear the hallmarks of Frances Warfield's journalistic skills as she converts the incidents of her life into anecdotes filled with the tension of the diagnosis of hearing loss, the drama of adapting to her hearing impairment, the grief of disappointment, self-deprecatory humor as she stumbles from mishap to mayhem, and even a Hollywood-style happy ending in each memoir—a marriage proposal in the first one and the restoration of her hearing through surgery in the second one. Warfield writes of her shame at being deaf, her attendance at lipreading classes, her assessment of the classes, her panic at what being deaf would mean to her life, and her flirtation with a man in the corridor outside the classroom while hiding the fact of her deafness from him. She shows the power of words to carry an emotion beyond their intended meaning: "In the normal hearing world, deaf was still a four letter word. Impaired hearing in 1948 remained as it was in 1933 when I began my revolt: It wasn't quite nice." Here, I caught a glimpse into what it must have been like for my parents to discover my deafness in late 1957, almost three years after my birth. The delayed click of life's chance meant that I was not snapped into an earlier time of a segregated life, but was caught at the margins of a modern time—a time of oralism, integration, mainstreaming, and all the other possibilities of a deaf-hearing life. She also writes with the activist's desire to educate the reader, born of her keenness to share her insights with as many people as possible about the benefits of managing her hearing loss:

> Perhaps that was the chief thing I learned, during the 1930s, from lip reading. To hold my head up. It made a lot of difference. I was beginning to like myself a little bit better. I was beginning to like other people, for a change, instead of tying myself into knots trying to make them like me.

My face grew hot as my words rushed ahead of my thoughts. In my haste to impress on Damian the significance of my discovery of this writer, I struggled to string my words together in the right order. I tried to tell him how reading Frances Warfield's memoirs of her deaf life was like reading the letters of a much-loved aunt. Her spirit shone from the pages. I did not share her distaste for being deaf—she did not even like the word itself, preferring to say "hard of hearing" or "hearing loss." But Warfield's story reached out to me down through the panorama of years so vividly that I felt the warmth of an imagined friendship with her and the chill of its absence. The force of this realization had winded me. In quick succession, a wholly new realization blossomed: I had lived my life as an oral-deaf woman in keeping with my mother's hopes for me. She had no template for how to achieve her dreams, and so hacked out her own pathway on my behalf. I had benefited enormously from this, but similarly, *I* had no role model in the way of deaf elders and so I also had hacked out my own pathway, dodging this obstacle and that hurdle. Bumping into a wise deaf "elder" from time to time on that pathway might have been nice. Helpful even. The intensity with which I said these words provoked Damian to burst out in surprise, "You're emotional!" I flinched, laughed off his surprise, and changed the subject to lighter ground.

We stretched our coffees first into an hour and then slid into a second hour with another coffee each before we drew ourselves back into our real-world responsibilities. We smiled at each other as we parted ways, not daring to say too much, and when Damian asked, "Do you mind if I call you again?" I answered, "That would be lovely," and hoped that my heart had not revealed itself too shamelessly. I waited to hear from him. I held my counsel; did not confide in anyone at all, too bruised even to give voice to my disappointment. In any case, I did not feel entitled to be disappointed. "It was just a coffee date," I reminded myself.

January passed and my wall calendar showed a picture of a Sunshine Coast beach in February. I kept myself busy with weekends away at the beach with friends and with work projects at the university during the weekdays, and then, during a birthday celebration dinner at a restaurant, I saw Damian. My cheeks felt like two hard little puddings as I shaped a smile at him across the tables separating us. He straightened his back and briefly closed his eyes as if to erase the image of me clear from his retinas; on opening his eyes, his returning smile held the warmth of a salesman. Yet, as I was leaving the restaurant alone at the end of the evening, after saying goodbye to my friends and clutching a bundle of birthday gifts, Damian broke away from his dinner companions, strode over to me, and asked if I would like a lift home with him. It was no trouble, he said; he didn't mind going out of his way. In a churning whirl of hope and helplessness, I let myself be driven home from my birthday dinner by Damian, me straining to keep up my end of the conversation and he chatting away brightly about this and that.

The darkness inside the car, the burr of the passing traffic, and the glitter of the night lights along the riverbank all conspired to create a mood of intimacy, but that mood dropped into the chill of a prison cell as soon as Damian pulled up outside my home. His bright chat snapped off with the abruptness of a pulled plug, and with his hands holding tightly onto the steering wheel, he looked straight ahead through the windscreen. His split-second change from sunniness to surliness bewildered me. I tried to break the tension by calling on all my convent-schooled manners, and said, "Thank you for driving me home. It was lovely to see you again." Still looking ahead as if standing to attention on military parade, he was terse. "I can't do this." I frowned at him, tongue-tied. The silence filled the car. I kept watching him. Damian dropped his hands onto his lap and turned sideways to the steering wheel so that he could face me squarely. He reached for my hands and, holding them in a prayerlike clasp, said in a voice thick with effort, "I'm sorry I can't be the person you want me to be." We said more words; he to me, me to him, and sometimes one or the other of us to the night air as if to call on the support of a third, unseen person. I was torn between being cynical, and cutting him to the quick, or throwing a hissy fit, but in the end, I was too hurt to argue any further, to bargain, or plead my case. There was no point, and nor was there any point in my hurting him in retaliation. Instead, I leant over the gear stick between us, kissed his cheek, and got out of his car, bundling up my purse and birthday presents in an awkward embrace.

When I reached the front door of my home, I turned back just in time to see Damian's arm extended toward me through the passenger window in a wave, but I could not see his face. I stepped across the threshold of my home and closed the door.

I shivered and curled up my toes against the pain tearing through my chest. In the solitariness of my bedroom, I cajoled myself, "I can get through this." I repeated these words mantralike, until they swayed into the rhythm of the rosary, all the syllables running together, their comfort arising from their rise and fall, that hypnotic lull of the chant. I fell asleep with the promise to myself that I would telephone a counselor the next morning. It was time, once and for all, to stop yearning for the prospect of romantic love and to start learning how to live a loving life as a single woman.

16

All Grown Up Now

Getting over Damian took some time. As usual, work was a good antidote. Over the next few months, I kept myself busy with a teaching gig at a university and took on a writing project for a major commercial management company. My friends helped me with other distractions: I swam up and down the pool each weekend; went for late afternoon rambles along the Sandgate foreshore; hiked up Mount Glorious, huffing and puffing and grabbing at my knees to catch my breath; and hosted Sunday lunches on the balcony of my apartment.

I also read more books about deafness: two by deaf academics in the United States, and two by novelists, one English and the other American. In *Writing Deafness*, Christopher Krentz wrote about the ways nineteenth-century American deaf and hearing writers thought about deafness. His description of "the hearing line, that invisible boundary separating deaf and hearing people" warmed me with its familiarity, despite its specter of separation. (I also discovered the correct meaning of the word "antebellum." For some reason, I had always thought it was a type of fabric, perhaps a suede-leather-like concoction; maybe of French origin. It's not, of course; I had confused it with vellum. Antebellum is a historical term referring to the period before the American Civil War. Odd, how one can get a fixed idea about the meaning of words simply by the lilt and tilt of their vowels.) Christopher Jon Heuer's mordant humor about his hearing loss in his anthology of essays, *BUG: Deaf Identity and Internal Revolution*, startled me. I laughed and felt uncomfortable at the same time. Heuer is dismissive of the difficulties others might have with his chaotic, conflict-embracing approach: "Deal with it." The English writer David Lodge's semiautobiographical novel, *Deaf Sentence,* and Philip Zazove's family-saga novel, *Four Days in Michigan*, set side by side, provide a study of extremes. Both Lodge and Zazove have a hearing loss. Lodge's loss is age-related, while Zazove has been deaf since childhood. Lodge approaches deafness as a hateful and humiliating impairment, which he attacks with self-pitying humor. I'm not a fan; maybe I'm overstating things, but I didn't like the undertone of sneering at deafness that seeps through in Lodge's novel. In contrast, Zazove took me on a Frommer's tour of historical and contemporary deaf family life, deaf politics, the inequities of deaf education, religious cultures, North American history with its melting-pot immigrant culture, and Washington politics. I got to know Zazove's vivacious fictional families so well that I wanted to meet them.

I enjoyed thinking of myself as a member of a diaspora of deaf writers. All these things were restorative in their power, drawing me away from my sadness.

During this healing time, on Sunday, April 6, 2008, four of my childhood deaf friends came to lunch at my home: Sharon, Jennifer, Kay, and her husband Kenneth. It rained heavily that day, a drought-breaking rain of near-biblical proportions. The gutters overflowed and flooded some streets, causing delays in the traffic. Kay and Kenneth arrived on time despite the chaos, followed not long after by Jennifer, and finally Sharon (who had taken a wrong turning off the motorway) arrived in a fluster of apologies. "I'm wet!" she laughed, shaking herself down. They were all cheerful about getting drenched in the race from their cars to my front door; the drama of rain, umbrellas, and damp hair was a happy distraction for us. I skittered about, foisting glasses of wine and fruit juice onto my guests, and saw that their faces reflected my keenness for everything to go well for this reunion lunch. We watched the rain for a while, letting it guide our talk until we found the ease of our bearings with each other again.

Over our plates of salad, barbecue chicken, and zucchini tart, our conversation dipped in and out of memories of our Deaf School days. Rose-tinted glasses colored our stories as we spoke with affection about our teachers and their quirks. Sharon remembered Mrs. Mason's crafts lessons; Kay said, "I've still got the plastic beaded coat hangers and place mats from those classes!" They recalled Mr. Thomas with the force of smitten love that children reserve for their favorite teacher, but I had left the Deaf School by then and did not know him. The memories darkened when Jennifer remarked on a teacher who took the preschool classes. "She told my mother there was no point teaching me. I was four years old. I'd just had an operation on my heart. She said to my mother, 'With her weak heart, she will not live long enough to benefit from our teaching.'" We fell momentarily silent; it was an impossible thing to countenance. Sharon, Kay, and Jennifer had more stories to tell from those long-ago days than I did. Perhaps this was because they had stayed on at the Deaf School for a year or so longer than I had, or maybe it was because they had seen each other regularly all through their adulthood and so were more practiced in reviving their recollections. Kenneth was content to listen, offering a comment here and a question there to push things along. We were like old soldiers of war in the way we told and retold our stories of the Deaf School days, polishing and embellishing the details to get them just right.

Our reminiscences shifted gears: we talked about what being deaf meant to each of us. The others knew I was searching for a better understanding of how my deafness had shaped my life, and they were keen to be part of this search. Kay had even prepared for this conversation by bringing along copies of old school reports and pages of typed-up notes recording her own insights. Like Sharon, Kay was profoundly deaf (although she described herself as "hard of hearing") and spoke rather than signed. She was a reflective woman who, on realizing some twenty years after she left her mainstream school that she had not received the education she deserved and was capable of, undertook an ambitious reading program to make up for lost time. She had forgone her childhood ambition to be a nurse: she was told that her deafness meant this was not a realistic option and instead, had chosen to do office work, which she loved, along with marriage and children. Kenneth, a former electronics technician at a university, was partially deaf and spoke with a clipped accent. "Some people ask me if I'm Scottish," he said, raising his eyebrows at the absurdity of it.

"I *like* noise!" Sharon said. "I put my hearing aid on as soon as I wake up, and I don't take it off again until I'm in bed." Jennifer and I caught each other's eyes, shook our heads, and Jennifer said, "No. Quiet is better." Sharon was insistent. She told of having her hearing aid stolen when she was at the beach—she had taken it off and put it in a bag while she went for a surf—and how she erupted into tears of frustration when the audiologist said that it would take several days to provide a new one for her. "It was awful," she said. I remembered my own panic at the beach and knew her feeling of awfulness.

When Kay said she did not like the sound of her own voice, we looked at her in surprise. "What? Why do you say that?" She grimaced. "People say my voice is too nasally." We could not dissuade her, and she went on, "I sometimes feel when hearing people tell me that I speak well, it is either a way of them telling me that I must not be too deaf or it is a condescending way of patting me on the back for trying to squeeze my square voice into the proverbial round hole. Growing up, I always got mixed messages about my speech and speaking skills. My teachers and adults would always praise the way I spoke or make a big deal out of it, but my peers always told me that I talked funny. They said they had trouble understanding me and that I talked through my nose. So why did the adults and teachers tell me different?" It was a long speech; she did not usually talk at such length. She looked downcast and fiddled with her napkin. In an effort to cheer her up, Sharon said, "Oh well, I think my voice is too soft. I wish it was stronger and louder," but Kenneth objected, "You've got a sexy voice!" Sharon blushed at this and giggled when Kay, Jennifer, and I teased her, "Oh yes, you do!"

Jennifer spoke about her decision to use sign language when she was a student in a mainstream high school even though she could speak well. It was a brave thing to do; she had to overcome her mother's opposition. A deaf person's ability to speak well is not necessarily a meal ticket to easy conversation with a hearing person; it can even be a hindrance because the hearing person is likely to underestimate the degree of effort that is required by the deaf person to achieve such fluency. This type of misunderstanding will be familiar to anyone who has attended foreign language classes—say, French or Italian or Japanese—in preparation for an extended holiday overseas. You arrive at your holiday destination straining at the bit to say "Un café au lait, s'il vous plaît," or "Buongiorno, quanto costa?" or "Konnichiwa, arigato," and then panic at the word storm that follows when the French waiter, Italian shop assistant, or Japanese receptionist greets your linguistic efforts with a flurry of chat in their native language. When they have drawn breath to await your reply, you swallow your disappointment, and you either pull out your language phrase book or, as is more likely, resort to your childhood gift of playing charades. The gestures of mimicry come back to you in full flight, and there you stay— in the land of gesture —until you come back home. And so it comes about that many deaf people either tire of the relentless effort to remain fluent in the world of oral languages or make the political decision to challenge head-on the daily onslaught of ignorance, incomprehension, or lack of courtesies. (Face the person being spoken to, keep the room lights switched on high, don't be snappish or roll your eyes with impatience at the deaf person.) Jennifer's fluency first, in Signed English (sign language that matches the spoken order of English) and later in Auslan (a visual-spatial language with its own grammar), gave her more chances to do what she wanted to do, beyond what she might have achieved without that second language. Despite Jennifer's enthusiasm for signed communication, Sharon, Kay, Kenneth, and I remained sheepish in our lack of skill for it. I had only completed one semester of Auslan with Jennifer. I would have to do several more years of study to become proficient. We begged off learning it now, crying out, "We're too old! It's too hard!"

(That evening after everyone had gone home, I sat on the edge of my bed to read Kay's typed-up notes and found where she had summed up the dilemma that confronted all our parents—not just Jennifer's mother—when we were children: "When we all left to go to various hearing schools, our speech improved but we were unhappy in our educational surroundings. On the other hand, if we had stayed on at the deaf school for all the rest of our school days, it's possible our oral communication would have suffered but we might have been happy in that particular environment in our deaf circle. It was a choice we were not old enough to make but I know my parents made the decision easily: no sign language for me." The crispness of her words stung, made my chest tight, she was right; but I was glad my parents chose speech for me.)

None of us were keen on the idea of cochlear implants for ourselves. We agreed that if we were given the option to have one, we would not take it up at this stage of our lives. We had no motivation, such as might stir us if we lost *all* sound entirely, to seek it out. Our consensus was not driven by hostility to new technology: I had read somewhere that even when the first "wearable" hearing aids were introduced, there were protests that deaf people were being turned into robots. Nor were we stirred into outrage that our deaf identity might be under threat. After all, the cochlear implant was really just a fancy hearing aid worn *inside* the skull rather than outside; it didn't take your deafness away; you still had to manage all the stuff that comes from relying on technology to boost your performance in the world of oral speech. It was more that we accepted what we had; for all the difficulties we had with keeping our conventional hearing aids tuned, dry, and out of the range of thieves, they would do. We gained enough benefit from our aids to get by. We were also squeamish about the surgical intervention that is required. "Besides," Sharon said, "If I had a cochlear implant, I would have to hear the noises at night when I turn the lights out and go to bed. That would be too spooky!" We laughed at her, and Jennifer explained, "You can turn the cochlear implant off," but Sharon was still doubtful. Kay and Jennifer knew deaf mothers who had chosen to have their deaf toddler-aged children implanted with cochlear hearing devices. We chewed the fat about how difficult this decision must have been, how the mothers must have worried about being judged by some of their deaf friends. They would have relied on their conviction that being able to hear early in life would increase their children's probability of having clear speech and comprehension, buffering them against discrimination and expanding their life choices in all sorts of ways.

Our mood lightened when Sharon piped up, "Remember the dancing lessons?" Yes! We grinned at each other as Kenneth held out his arms in the dancer's position, one arm curved higher than the other, and mimed how we placed our little feet on Mr. Pritchard's shoes as he bore our weight in time to music, unheard by us. Those dancing lessons! The joy of them! Sandi had remembered them too.

I did not talk much during the lunch, partly because I was absorbed by my hostess duties but mainly because I wanted to concentrate on what the others had to say. Kay and Kenneth commented on my reserve while they helped me to clear the dishes off the table. Kay said, "Perhaps you are trying to remember everything we have said, but maybe you will tell us more about yourself when we get together again." Kenneth echoed her, "Yes, we want you to tell us what you are thinking. It takes time, I know, to do this." He repeated his wish, the one he had expressed to me a few months earlier. "You must write your story because it's our story too." I was moved by their concern. I had already come to understand, as I sat at the lunch table watching my childhood deaf friends chat, how they had always been an important part of my life even if we had not been present to each other for most of it. We were bound by our unique insider knowledge: just as deaf people cannot understand what hearing people can hear, so hearing people cannot understand what deaf people experience. In particular, unlike the hearing members of our families, we knew the effort of moving back and forth across the hearing line, the invisible border that does double-duty in separating and joining our deaf and hearing selves.

When I went to the reunion get-together organized by Jennifer before I traveled to England a few years earlier, I had been overwhelmed by her generosity in doing this for me; but that occasion had been held at a café and while I was the "guest of honor," I had felt more like a visitor parachuting in from another country. This time, my lunch, though small with just five of us, was initiated and hosted by me. Having welcomed my friends into my home, I was welcoming them back into my life. It felt like an act of repatriation. This sounds dramatic, but I cannot help that. Later, I realized that our lunch was exactly a year after I began my "deaf project" with an entry in my journal on Good Friday, April 6, 2007, "Today, I begin . . ." It was just a coincidence, but I liked the serendipity of it.

All the same, my reunion lunch left me subdued for several days, and I still recall it with a "pinging" sensation, that pluck of the heart and the contraction of the stomach when you see the choices laid out clearly before you. It is one thing to have lunch with your friends reminiscing about the good old days. It is quite another thing altogether when you are given glimpses into their hardships and know that you have the ability to act, not necessarily on their behalf, because they are more than capable of doing so for themselves, but on behalf of those who cannot. I had discovered much during the course of my exploration into my deaf life, and I had repeatedly promised myself to "do something" with what I had learned, especially when I witnessed the leadership of people such as my former housemate and now prominent deaf academic, Bridget, and my deaf activist pen pal, Michael. Just as often, I had let my promise slip away in the tide of distractions. I resolved, once more, to "do something."

A year after that lunch on the balcony of my home with Sharon, Jennifer, Kay and Kenneth, I visited the Rochester National Technical Institute for the Deaf, in upstate New York, for three days. The warmth of the hospitality was overwhelming. I met with academics, deaf and hearing; gave a presentation to an audience of academics and students, again deaf and hearing, on the topic of deaf identity based on my own search for a better understanding of the relationship between my deaf-self and my hearing persona; and walked around the campus, where I watched the students and academics, rugged up against the ice-cold air and snow-deep paths, talking with each other in both American Sign Language and spoken American English. Even the hearing wait-staff in the campus cafeterias signed, when required, to their deaf customers.

From the first moment, I was bedazzled. I fell into a swoon of wonderment, felt the buzz of "wow!" Even though I could not use American Sign Language, I understood, at last, a long-ago comment by Bridget: "You don't really know what acceptance is until you experience it." I understood, too, Oliver Sacks's enthusiasm for Gallaudet University, the same enthusiasm that I had once derided as sentimental and excessive, while also admitting to a renegade pang of yearning. In Rochester, I felt completely at home in that university for deaf students, on the other side of the globe from my home in Australia.

When I was invited to return there to teach, I accepted with a glad heart. And then the next thing happened.

In the final stages of writing this memoir of deafness, I was diagnosed with non-Hodgkins lymphoma, a cancer of the blood. I was relieved to be told the news; it explained the persistent bouts of fatigue and petty illnesses, such as the minor head cold morphing into what I had jokingly named "the twelve-week flu." I was daunted by the proposed treatment plan, which required six doses of chemotherapy over a period of four months. A stem cell transplant was also mentioned. I wondered how I was going to fit the treatment sessions in between everything else in my life. I proposed an idea—Black Adder–like, a cunning plan—to Doctor Frost, the hematologist. "How about we wait for a few months before I start the chemo?" He looked over his spectacles at me. His response was mild. "I don't think so. We'll start you off next Thursday," and he handed over a green and white booklet called "Understanding Lymphomas." I flipped through the booklet on the way out of his room and was critical of its design layout, color scheme, typeface, and corny cartoons. The black text smudged its way across the pages, absent of any meaning.

I sat in my car in the car park beneath the medical center and wondered what my first step ought to be. I obviously had to tell someone, but who?

Not my mother; she had enough to worry about. Not my sister; she had plenty to deal with too, and besides, she was going away on a holiday to Carnarvon Gorge the next day. No point telling her. I went through my list of friends. Nope, couldn't tell any of them, they were all busy with family and work as well. I was stumped. I sat in the car and drummed my fingers on the steering wheel. I couldn't decide what to do. Still undecided, I turned the ignition on and drove out of the car park—oops, in the wrong lane; nearly collided with that four-wheel drive—and headed toward home. My mother. My sister. My friends. My mind tumbled in a spin-cycle mode, and then snapped off at the "my mother" switch; I pulled up at a curb and called my sister, but her mobile phone rang out, and so I drove to my mother's home to tell her the news.

Saying the words to my mother that Doctor Frost had said to me and watching my mother's face as she absorbed the news had a tugging effect. I blinked back my first tears and tightened my stomach against a sea-sick motion of fright. My mother hugged me. Her small face looked full. "We'll take care of you. Everyone's here for you. You won't have to worry about anything at all." I nodded, said, "Thanks. That'll be good." I drove home, rang the dentist to confirm an appointment and on being asked to wait, tears broke from me, and I shouted at Jade, the receptionist, told her she was incompetent and demanded to speak to her manager, and no, I wouldn't hold on, she could bloody well go and get the manager right now because I was not going anywhere, no bloody way was I going to wait for a second longer, I had to have chemotherapy next week, so there, and so what was she going to do about that, hey? I wheezed and sniffled my way to a halt; let myself be consoled by Jade, who was schooled in grace. I put the phone down. It rang. It was my sister. We chatted; I told her the news; she stalled momentarily before regrouping, knew it would all be fine, everything would go well, did I say Doctor Frost? She knew about him, he was great, she was going away, I knew that didn't I? Well, I could e-mail her, her mobile phone would be out of range, but I could e-mail her, I had her e-mail address, here it is again anyway just in case I didn't. I said that Carnarvon Gorge would be cold; I would pop around with my merino wool wrap for her to take away with her. It's a nice color, I said, charcoal grey, you will feel cozy and glamorous. Only if you've got time, she said. I said I had time.

The rest of the day passed in the usual haze of postdiagnosis confusion, and I did what I always did when under stress; I worked. I finished a report about a disability seminar I had organized for my client, a peak organization for vocational education and training, and finalized preparations for meetings the next week. With that out of the way, I looked around my home, wandering from room to room. A late afternoon glow washed the rooms in warmth. I stood before the Luke Wagner landscape paintings on the walls; touched the tips of the pink and white flowers in their vases; brushed against the glossy art and travel books stacked on the coffee table, and trailed my fingers along the other books pushed into shelves all around me. I sat down on the chesterfield; its pale green and rose-pink tapestry upholstery and brown wood panels inserted in each arm, just large enough to rest a glass of wine, conjured up a well-mannered era of five o'clock cocktails, gathered skirts, and cigarettes held up high, at a certain angle, in long-stemmed holders. My eyes fell on a bank of photos on the walnut-colored sideboard. Sharon and I smiled in one shot; Rose and I laughed out of another frame. That gave me an idea. "I'll give Rose a call. See what she's got to say."

I phoned Rose. Told her. Dismay. Words of comfort and courage. Difficult to say who was doing the comforting and 'couraging, we both were. My other phone rang. It was Simon, my once-upon-a-time, would-be-deaf-if-he-could nephew, now a man of twenty-seven years. Rose said she would call back. Simon and I spoke. I put the phone down. It rang again. It was my niece, Jessica. We spoke. I put the phone down again. Emma rang. We spoke. Rose rang back. We spoke, her mother sent her love. I put the phone down. It rang again. Jason, Simon's brother, this time. We spoke. I put the phone down. Rose rang back, did I want to go over for dinner? No? That's okay. Liz rang. Kris e-mailed. So did Jenny and Ian. Maria and Tony too. Bronnie called. And so it went, for the next day, and in the days and the nights and the new days following. Phone calls and e-mails from my friends, all carrying their words of love, all rostering themselves to drive me to the hospital, sit with me, pick me up, take me home, cook meals, and chivvying me to do what must be done.

Their practical care shaped my hopes. It might have been shock, it might have been naiveté, it might have been foolishness, but on that first night of sleeplessness, I felt as if I had been washed in spring waters with the astringency of peppermint. I saw what lay ahead for me. I would endure twelve difficult months—I wasn't thrilled about this, but I would tackle it as if it was another ocean swim race, try not to be pulled under by the riptides, swing one arm over the other until I could surf into the beach on the final breaking waves and run toward my waiting friends—but at the end of that time, I would be well. I would honor my private promise to my son Jack, the one in which I undertook to outlive both my parents. I would return to the Rochester National Technical Institute for the Deaf to teach in their spring semester. I would then come back home, where I would work for the best educational opportunities for deaf students in Australia, and I would write, laugh, and love my family and all my friends, deaf and hearing, all the while.

17

A Reluctant Memoirist

Other than being deaf, my life is not especially unusual. In this way, I am both ordinary and singular. My life has been pitted here with deep sadness and lifted there with joy, but it has been mostly a plateau held stable by the grist of daily routines. But when I am asked about my deafness, I feel myself tilting—just a little, but it's there—outside the support of those routines. The questions may be polite or they may be intrusive, but they always act as a trigger for me to be wary. According to my mood at any given moment, I have resisted, objected to, evaded, and even answered those questions. As a child, I complained to my mother; as an adult, I bristled and prickled. A lifetime of such questions congealed into one big lump when that long-ago psychologist half-stated, half-asked me with the sureness of somewhat who felt the advantage of being a hearing person, "Your deafness, it must have a big impact on your life?"

While writing my memoir of deafness, I learned my mother was right when she said, "Just answer their questions. They are interested, they just want to know." Today, I am still obeying my mother and still answering other people's questions. But the questions about my deafness that I most needed to answer were my own. Until I set out on my search to understand my deaf-self, I did not give voice to the questions *I* wanted to ask. I held them close, not giving myself permission or granting myself the nerve to explore, test, and perhaps even drop long-standing habits of understanding myself. Now, as this is a memoir of deafness—*my* memoir by which I aim to *own* my story, as well as tell it—I must persevere with the final task of pulling together the threads of my new understanding.

I had a confused relationship with my deafness. I could live with this, but it created a minefield for others to negotiate. I came reluctantly to the task of getting a handle on the meanings of my deaf experiences, my deafness, and my "being deaf." I made several false starts in my exploration. I could not understand what was holding me back from finding, and then telling, my story of deafness. I thought for a while that this reluctance was because I felt threatened by the task and I wondered why this should be so. My fears had nothing to do with shame or the desire to disown my deaf status. They sprang from my experiences and observations: I saw, with slivers of anger lodged in my heart and curdled fright rumbling in my stomach, how many hearing people treat and talk about deaf people, and I nursed the fear that *I* might also be treated and talked about in such a way, with devastating consequences: lessened career prospects, compromised friendships, and conditional love. In a tiny, dark, and faraway corner of my heart was also the fear that perhaps I *was* a lesser person in some way, because here I was, routinely inconveniencing so many people because I couldn't hear properly and didn't say every word properly. Admitting this fear to myself, let alone to anyone else, was hard.

When I realized my silence was acting as a brake on my ability to live authentically, and as a brake on other people's understanding of the variety of possibilities for deaf people's lives, I shook off my restraint. In writing my memoir of deafness, I was finally "doing" that "something" that I needed to do. Writing woke me up from my passivity about my deafness. I understood that by sharing my story of deafness, I was adding to the knowledge of deaf lives as told by deaf people, rather than as "explained" by people who can hear. I was also adding to a repository of images of deaf people. My memoir is not intended to be representative of deaf people's lives: how can it be? I cannot experience the deafness (or hearingness, for that matter) of others, and I have struggled to understand the impact of my own deafness on my life, let alone other people's deafness.

Whatever the reader's response to my memoir, it is useful that this particular image of a deaf life is available, alongside the diversity of other deaf stories, because otherwise, how do we know who we are—or test who we can be—if we never see ourselves reflected in what is written? Just as important, how do *others* understand us if our stories about deafness and what it means to be deaf are missing from what they read? How do hearing parents of deaf children guide their young children's lives if they do not have an array of life stories from deaf adults from which to learn? From which to cherry-pick this experience and reflect upon that insight, weaving them into their own instincts about the best thing to do for their children.

I gave myself over to the mission of remembering, describing, clarifying, defining, and interpreting my experiences of deafness in response to the psychologist's question and to all the other questions that lay behind it. This was a ragged, tearing, and chiseling experience leavened at first with only occasional moments of joy, but as the race toward my mission's end drew nearer, I noticed a growing sense of ease within myself and with my life.

However, I still quailed at the prospects of breaching my own privacy as well as intruding upon the privacy of others. I did not want my memoir to be an exercise in disability tourism for the curious, but merely idle, reader. I was mindful of the "catch 22" involved in opening up my life to the gaze of others. My parents' benchmark for my "success" as a deaf woman was the degree to which I blended in with, and integrated into, the hearing world. Yet, to answer the questions of others about my deafness, I had to step outside that world. Given that personal privacy was being sacrificed, I wanted my memoir to matter, to grab the reader's attention and give them pause to reflect, to wonder, and ask even more questions to bring about an improved understanding of the lives and needs of deaf people.

One thing was certain right from the start. I would not, could not, and refused to frame my memoir as a "triumph over adversity" narrative. Nor did I want my book to be a "tell all," a trauma account, or a "pity-party," as a colleague crisply warned. I do not know if I have succeeded in this aim. I resisted these approaches for several reasons.

First, I understood my external experiences of *deafness* to have been largely a series of adaptations to specific incidents ranging from the hurtful and irritating to the difficult and outrageous, rather than an uninterrupted struggle against hardship. At the same time, my inner sense of myself as *"being deaf"* has been mostly sanguine.

Second, the "triumph over adversity" memoir usually starts with the certain premise that life was good until some terrible thing happened. The memoir then unfolds as a series of dire consequences and apparently insurmountable obstacles against which the heroic writer successfully battles. The memoirist's character emerges as a survivor. In contrast, the narrative arc of my life has been, and continues to be, less apparent. My struggles have had less to do with the specific auditory detail of my deafness and more to do with the general questions of life that confront all of us.

Third, and perhaps most significant, my deafness emerged fully formed with my birth, and so I did not experience that cataclysmic fracture between "hearing" and "no hearing" described so vividly by other memoirists who became deaf through illness or trauma. The unfolding of my story is not about conquering battles, but about inviting the reader into my world to see what it feels and sounds like. My search is not limited to understanding my deafness, but extends to understanding the nature of my relationships with others, including the search for love.

I understand that my mother may regard me as her triumph because she established the foundations for my deaf-hearing life with all its opportunities according to her vision and hopes for me. However, I do not regard myself, or my life, as a triumph simply by dint of succeeding as a deaf woman in the hearing world.

My early life was shaped by the exertion of my mother's will so that I gained the necessary competencies to participate fully as a deaf woman in the hearing world. As an unreflective and usually compliant accomplice to my mother's will, my introspection about my deaf life was fitful. I was rarely animated by any sense of deaf politics or deaf identity. I scurried among my memories and then let them fade. I didn't attribute any significance to my memories, because I thought their private nature precluded them from having a public purpose. By and large, I was happy enough to go along with the family line: I was a deaf girl made good.

I made little effort to understand myself—or others—in relation to my deafness. This is not necessarily a bad thing. How many hearing people embark on an exploration of the meaning of their hearing or indeed, *any* elements of their lives that might mark them out as "different" or "other," to the quality of their lives? My long-standing indifference toward articulating the meaning of my deafness could be read as a default acceptance of my deafness. It could be seen as proof that, by and large, I got on with things, just as my parents had hoped that I would.

My exploration of my relationship with my deafness entailed separating myself from my mother's will. This task is not peculiar to deaf people. All children need to undertake the adult task of separating from their parents, but it is possibly more apparent for deaf children, especially those who are born into hearing families. I had to stake out the private essence of my hearing persona/deaf identity.

The one thing I was always certain about was this: I was content to declare myself as deaf. "Deaf." Whether it's read on the page or said out loud, it's a short word that carries an explosive power, but it was never a word I shied away from. The strength of my feeling about this is undiminished, even though I have lived my life predominantly as a "hearing-deaf" person. But there is no getting away from the central issue: I am deaf. It is as simple as that for me. At the same time, it is not so simple because my deafness is essential to my sense of I-am-who-I-am. It is not just an auditory attribute.

My deafness is more than the backdrop to my sense of self; it is the context in which I am located. When a friend asked me whether I ever think that I am *not* deaf, that I *can* hear, it's just that I need a machine to sustain my hearing ability, I was emphatic. "I always know I am deaf. Always." However—and herein lies the twist that I cannot quite explain away—I do not like being regarded by others as a "deaf woman" as if I possess no other qualities, and nor do I like it when people try to "take away" my deafness with comments such as "You seem just like a hearing person." This grates. I want to be recognized in all my complexity, not as an organism of failed auditory nerves. My private, nonnegotiable insistence on being understood by others in a layered, textured, multidimensional way has restrained me from publicly staking out my identity as a "deaf woman."

I attacked the task of writing *The Art of Being Deaf* with the conviction that I had something positive to say and demonstrate about my deaf life, but as the project proceeded, I stumbled. In the absence of my deaf friends or mentors, and in the climate of my own reluctance to discuss my concerns with hearing people who, when I flagged any anxieties about issues arising from my deafness, tended to be hearty and upbeat in their responses, I had to work things out for myself.

This is why historical and contemporary novels with deaf characters and memoirs by deaf writers were such useful guides for my reflections on my deaf life and deaf-self. We must all take our sense of connectedness from where we can best find it. For some deaf people, it is within their own Deaf community. For others such as myself—those "shadow-land" oral-deaf people scattered across the hearing world—such a sense of connectedness can be buried or lost. Being able to access the heritage of deaf memoirs, biographies, and life narratives was enormously helpful to me. I felt the hand of mentoring reach down to me across the span of history.

Reading deaf narratives while writing my memoir changed my self-concept as a deaf woman. I enjoyed the companionability of it, but only once I got over my fright at seeing so many different documented versions of deaf experiences, and it *was* a fright. For a while there, it was like walking through the Hall of Mirrors in Luna Park. Did I *really* look like that? Or no, perhaps I was like *that*? When I stopped searching for the right mirror, the single defining portrait, I enjoyed seeing my deaf-self/hearing-persona experiences reflected in, or challenged by, what I read. The fictional imaginings by hearing and deaf writers of deaf characters, the observations of biographers of deaf people, and the recollections of deaf memoirists cast my own memories in new lights. I considered my experiences more contemplatively and less reactively than I might otherwise have done. When reading those novels and memoirs, I thought too, how I might change people's understanding of deaf lives rather than just read and comment on it.

In surmising how my day-to-day relationships might have been affected by my deafness, I saw that in my childhood, my deafness was contained within many borders. Some of these borders were obvious: my entire extended family was hearing and so served as a stronghold against any encroachment by the deaf community. Their enthusiasm for every advance that I made in my deaf-hearing life had the power of a shamanic talisman, warding off the threat that *being deaf* might overtake my life. Many suburbs and a wide wending river lay between my childhood home and the school for deaf children and the homes of my deaf friends. Even the private girls' school I attended after an incubation period of five years at the Deaf School was protected by that same river and high stone walls.

As I grew into adulthood, a less apparent border moved into place: an invisible membrane, like porous cling-wrap, grew between my public deaf-in-the-hearing-world persona and my private deaf self. This membrane is permanent and so is the duality of my public "hearing-deaf" self and private deaf-self. The dominance of either the public or private self depends on the circumstances in which I find myself. Sometimes, I *feel* deaf, such as when someone mocks my speech (this happens more often than you might imagine, and it still hurts); or openly *declare* myself to be deaf, such as when I ask for the lights to be turned on high in a room full of people. At other times, my deafness lies dormant within me while I get on with the routines of my daily life.

I have written earlier about the epiphany a close university friend experienced on reading about my terror in a storm blackout. She had also written in her letter,

> I tried hard to focus my earliest memories of meeting you and knowing you, and the best memories that I could come up with did not define you by deafness. . . . I suppose I will never think of you as deaf, because that is not how you wanted to introduce yourself all those years ago.

I was touched by her honesty, but puzzled as well. I had never intended my deafness to be an unspeakable secret, and yet here I was confronted with evidence that this was exactly how I presented myself. I showed the letter to another good friend, one who had seen me at my worst and at my best and at other times in between. When she said that this had been her experience of me as well, I reacted badly to this second confession. I snapped, "What? Do you expect me to be Deaf Studies 101? Am I supposed to download everything I know and feel about being deaf every time I meet someone?"

As I machine-gunned my anger at her, I realized this was the very same anger I had felt in response to the psychologist's question several years earlier. In the heat of that memory, I rushed on, my words and heart ablaze. "Why must I explain myself over and over again? There's always this assumption laid on people who are deaf or who have a disability that they are duty-bound to explain themselves. As if we are Exhibit A. Or a museum piece! You don't have to explain your hearingness to me or to anyone else for that matter. Why should I explain my deafness to you?"

My friend fought back. "Look, I get that being deaf is not the sum total of who you are. I also get that you want to be seen as someone for whom being deaf is no great drama, and that you have had other, more momentous issues in your life to contend with. Jack's death for one thing. Your cancer for another. And we've all been there for you during those times because we love you. We care about you. But I just cannot believe that the way people respond to your deafness has not been an important thing for you to deal with. I don't understand why you let us talk about these other important times in your life, but you don't give us any leeway to ask you about your deafness. You've had to show a lot of guts over the years. You should give yourself some credit. It's not all been about your mother's efforts. You've had to put in the hard yards too, and I can't help feeling that it's been a lonely experience for you sometimes."

I felt shaken by my friend's retaliatory words. They carried truths that I had not allowed myself to acknowledge. I bit my bottom lip to stop my emotions from rising to the surface. I shifted my gaze away from my friend, toward the lush tropical panorama of her back yard. The green, primeval-looking fronds of the palm trees jostled in the late afternoon breeze that was sweeping in from Moreton Bay. The silence was comfortable. Contemplative. Neither of us hurried to fill the gap.

Finally, I said, "Well, actually, I've always missed my childhood deaf friends, even while knowing the positive spin-offs from leaving the deaf school to go to All Hallows. It's sort of stayed with me as a gap. A missing-ness." My friend nodded and said, "You know, it's quite all right to admit that. You *have* had a lot of advantages because of your mother's advocacy for you, but there are trade-offs in every situation. There's usually a down-side in every positive scenario. The loss of your deaf friends in childhood was the downside to your getting that education your parents wanted for you." She repeated her conviction. "It's okay to allow yourself to feel sad about things. You don't have to be brave and stoic all the time!" We laughed to steady ourselves, and talked some more.

I told this friend, and I set it down here now, that I cannot imagine a life without my childhood deaf friends. It feels impossible to me. I had asked myself, in one of my moments of deep despondency, "Where are my childhood deaf friends?" I have discovered during the course of writing my memoir that they have always been present in my life, even if just by way of memories. It doesn't matter that I rarely see them anymore. It is enough for me to know that they are *there* and that I can call on them whenever I need to. Or even when I just feel like it. Having once run around play-grounds, painted on sheets of butcher's paper, and sat in classrooms with a clan of deaf children through my attendance for five years at the School for the Deaf, I will forever feel a kindred spirit with that clan. That kindred spirit locates me; gives me a sense of who I am. I don't have to explain myself to them.

My conviction about this was reinforced when I met a young Australian writer, Jessica White, who had recently moved to Brisbane, where I live. A former work colleague had told Jessica about me, given her my e-mail address, and suggested that she drop me a line. The words in Jessica's first e-mail to me could have been set to a dance tune; her words bounced along in a pull-and-push rhythm of excitement and apprehension. I agreed to meet her at one of the university cafes, where she explained that she is profoundly deaf in one ear and has some residual hearing in the other. She did not attend a special school for deaf children; her education choices were swept up in the tides of mainstreaming and integration. Jessica is gifted and works hard, enjoys the support of her family, and has earned academic and literary successes with her novels, *A Curious Intimacy* and *Entitlement*. (When I asked Jessica if she would ever write a novel about deafness, she said, "I would feel as though I was cheating in some way if I wrote about deaf people in my novels. I would feel too much as though I was writing about me.") She wanted to meet me because she had not known any deaf children when she was growing up and now did not know any other deaf people, let alone another deaf writer. As we sat across the iron-framed table from each other and chatted over our cups of coffee, I saw the attentiveness of Jessica's eyes on my face, and in that seeing, I saw how my eyes would be filled with the same attentiveness. Jessica was chatty and expressive. She smiled a lot; looked grave when thinking about something in particular; nodded every now and then; shook her head slowly once or twice in doubt. She interrupted herself several times to marvel at how unusual it was for her to speak with another deaf person. I was reminded that I too might have liked an older deaf mentor when I was young or just known a deaf adult somewhere on the fringes of my hearing-world life. Even now, as a woman in my fifties, I enjoy meeting older deaf women; conferences by deaf people are good occasions for this reason. I like to learn their stories, discover what their lives are like, and use them as touchstones of sorts.

Now I realize that one blue swallow does not make a summer. It is unwise to extrapolate from the isolated example of a young deaf woman navigating her way through the world "solo" as it were, but I cannot help musing about the value of my having that childhood deaf history to fall back on. I also reflect on the conversation I had with Maryanne Kelly, one of my teachers at the Deaf School. I had asked her what she thought about oralism, the method—or rather, a group of methods—of education that emphasizes spoken communication rather than signed language. She had smiled at me. "Well, you were the success story." And then she said it again, with a different emphasis, "Actually, you were *the* success story of oralism." Her frown hinted at some misgivings. "No doubt about that. Really, it just doesn't suit so many deaf children. I don't know what happens to them, now that there are no special schools for the deaf."

I don't know either. In any case, when I think about my life, I do not think of it as a "deaf life" or as a life in which I've done battle against the hearing world. My sense of deaf-self has expanded and contracted in tune with the erratic rhythms of my life's trajectory. My preoccupations have been, and continue to be, about love, friendships, and work. Not about my deafness. I resile the persistently held belief of others that my deafness has been my life's burden. It has not. I know about grief and the force of its power to pull you down. The sudden infant death of my son, Jack, taught me that. Still teaches me. And I know this too: Any grief I have experienced as a result of being deaf has been small when I measure it against my longing for my son. Perhaps the death of my son helps me to tap into the sorrow of those hearing parents who feel, even if ever-so-briefly that they dare not recognize it or confess it, that they have lost their son or daughter when they hear the words "Your child is deaf." These parents recover themselves to face the world and to do battle for their deaf child, but I sense their memory of that knifing news lies close beneath their skin. Their sorrow fuels their mission to give their deaf child the very best chance in the world. It is useful, this sorrow, but it is also contagious. It can seep into the skin of the child, infusing that child not with the grief of hearing loss but with the tension of uncertainty, of not quite knowing what to do to make everything all right. I am familiar with this anxiety. It courses through my days with the ease of a saline drip, but overflows from time to time as panicky, flustered attempts to right that which is wrong or in tearful shouting to make myself understood.

I don't believe that defining what makes us different from others is an especially useful way of explaining ourselves to each other. I prefer talking about the qualities that unify us, and I see that unity as residing in the intangibles of love, fear, loss, yearning, hope, loneliness, and all those soul elements that we have difficulty describing. I have found that when I talk about these intangibles to parents of deaf children as the elements that have shaped my life and my sense of who I am, they lean forward on their seats and their faces flicker with some sort of recognition. Their curiosity about my education, my career, my sense of spirituality, and my love of music is largely satiated, apart from a niggle here and there. It is loneliness and love, those universal questions we all struggle with, that they want to know more about. These parents also usually want to understand the reasons for my "success" in integrating into the hearing world where other deaf people have apparently failed. Who can answer such a loaded question with any real degree of precision? Especially when words like a "success" and "failure" can give rise to delusions about the power of individual effort. My best stab at an answer to this question is that I have been blessed with luck and opportunity, both brought to life through my parents' hopes and my own energy, combined with loads of tenacity and some courage, and the zeitgeist of the day.

In the end, my life is larger than my deaf-self. Each of us has a particular road to travel, with challenges or tasks to fulfil. My particular challenges have included being the daughter of an alcoholic father, and the bereaved mother of my son, Jack, and taking on the biggest task of all—the task of unconditional love. Each loss, disappointment, and sorrow has propelled me forward to tackle the next hurdle.

While writing this memoir, I have reconciled my childhood deaf self with my adult "hearing-deaf" persona. The two selves have merged as one. Coincidentally, while I wrote my way toward a better understanding of my hearing/deaf-self, my sadness about my romantic disappointments faded, giving way to a calmer appreciation of the love I give to, and receive from, my friends and family. I have found the sense of constancy that I thought being in a romantic relationship would give to me: the friend who told me all those years ago that constancy "comes from within" was right. The invisible membrane between my public hearing/deaf-self and my private deaf-self no longer feels like a wall to be guarded or scaled. I have relaxed my vigilance and am more at home with my deafness among all my friends, deaf and hearing. I have discovered the potency of love in all our lives and how it sustains us even during those times when we think it is absent.

I like to think, now, that maybe the art of being deaf is the art of life, which, of course, is the art of love. Having probed, dug up memories, and found some answers in response to the psychologist's question and to my own questions about my deaf experiences, I have new destinations to strike out toward, so much more to be discovered.

Epilogue: The Sleeper Awakes

She leant across the picnic hamper and reached for my hearing aid in my open-palmed hand. I jerked away from her, batting her hand away from mine. The glare of the summer sun blinded me. I struck empty air. Her tendril-fingers seized the beige seashell curve of my hearing aid and she lifted the cargo of sound toward her eyes. She peered at the empty battery-cage before flicking it open and shut as if it was a cigarette lighter, as if she could spark hearing-life into this trick of plastic and metal that held no meaning outside of my ear. I stared at her. A band of horror tightened around my throat, strangling my shout, "Don't do that!" I clenched my fist around the new battery that I had been about to insert into my hearing aid and imagined it speeding like a bullet toward her heart.

My heart raced as if I'd been running for my life. I swung my legs around to the side of my bed and pulled myself upright into wakefulness. The back of my neck was damp with perspiration. I waited for my agitation to subside and went to the bathroom to splash cold water onto my face. The mirror showed me that the whites of my eyes were stained red. I had been crying in the dream. I rested my forehead on the cold enamel of the bathroom sink.

Hearing aids are personal, intimate even. I protect them fiercely and rarely entrust them into the care of others, not even my closest friends. I certainly don't like other people touching my hearing aids. It is a shocking breach of intimacy, like exploring my ears, using the tips of their fingers to trace the outline of the vacuum where sound should echo. I don't even like people looking at them for any longer than passing curiosity warrants. The crude handling by the woman in the dream was nightmarish.

All the same, the ferocity of my reaction shook me. It made me stop and wonder. This dream was the first time in my life that I could recall being deaf in my dreams. Despite being born deaf and living in apparent harmony with my deafness all my life, my dream-self has no consciousness of being deaf. In my dreams, I hear sounds and conduct conversations with ease.

Two nights later, my deaf dream-self asserted itself again. This time I woke with a sense of marvel. My dream had taken me to a commemorative event at the Gladstone Road Oral Deaf School at Dutton Park, which I attended in my early childhood. I was surrounded by my deaf friends, some speaking and some signing, but all of us chatting and laughing. My attention was distracted by the arrival of a newcomer. As he approached the group, I saw that it was a friend who is not deaf. I called out to him with joy, "Hello! What are you doing here?" He smiled at me, "I wanted to see what your early life was like," and turning to greet my deaf friends, he signed his name, spelling it out letter by letter on his fingers with easy grace. His enthusiasm was infectious and prompted my friends to cluster around him, keen to teach him new signs.

These two dreams came while I was writing this memoir. I had already been reflecting and writing for several years about my relationship with my deaf-self and the impact of my deafness on my life, but I remained uneasy about writing about my deaf-life. I had lived all my adult life apart from the deaf community; belatedly casting myself as a deaf woman with something pressing to say about deaf people's lives felt absurd. The urgency to tell my story and my keenness to contest certain assumptions about deafness were real, but I was hampered by anxiety. I doubted my right to speak out. The dreams were potent, as if my deaf-self was not only asserting itself but also awakening me to the subtlety of the dance between my private deaf-self and my public deaf-hearing persona.

References Cited

Boyle, T. Coraghessan. *Talk Talk*. New York: Viking, 2006.

Caine, Hall. "The Scapegoat." In *The Quiet Ear: Deafness in Literature*, edited by Brian Grant. London: Deutsch, 1987.

Couser, G. Thomas. "Signs of Life: Deafness and Personal Narrative." In *Recovering Bodies: Illness, Disability, and Life Writing*. Madison: University of Wisconsin Press, 1997.

Cyrus, Bainy, E. Katz, C. Cheyney, and F. Parsons. *Deaf Women's Lives: Three Self-Portraits*. Washington DC: Gallaudet University Press, 2006.

Children of a Lesser God. New York: Paramount/CIC TAFT 1986. Videorecording.

Davis, Lennard J. *My Sense of Silence: Memoirs of a Childhood with Deafness*. Urbana and Chicago: University of Illinois Press, 2000.

Glennie, Evelyn. *Good Vibrations: My Autobiography*. London: Hutchinson, 1990.

Groce, Nora Ellen. *Everybody Here Spoke Sign Language: Hereditary Deafness on Martha's Vineyard*. Cambridge, MA, and London: Harvard University Press, 1985.

Heuer, Christopher Jon. *BUG: Deaf Identity and Internal Revolution*. Washington DC: Gallaudet University Press, 2007.

Itani, Frances. *Deafening*. New York: Grove Press, 2003.

Keller, Helen. *The Story of My Life*. New York: Doubleday, Page and Co., 1903.

————. *The World I Live In: edited and with an introduction by Roger Shat-tuck.* New York: New York Review Books Classics, 2003.

Kisor, Henry. *What's That Pig Outdoors?: A Memoir Of Deafness.* New York: Hill and Wang, 1990.

Krentz, Christopher. *Writing Deafness. The Hearing Line in 19th Century American Literature.* Chapel Hill: University of North Carolina Press, 2007.

Lodge, David. *Deaf Sentence.* London: Harvill Seeker, 2008.

Sacks, Oliver. *Seeing Voices.* London: Picador, 1991.

Seth, Vikram. *An Equal Music.* London: Phoenix House, 1999.

Stegner, Wallace. *Crossing to Safety.* London: Penguin Books, 2002.

Warfield, Frances. *Cotton in My Ears.* New York: Viking Press, 1948.

————. *Keep Listening.* London: Victor Gollancz Ltd., 1957.

White, Jessica. *A Curious Intimacy.* Australia: Penguin Books, 2008.

————. *Entitlement.* Australia: Penguin Books, 2012.

Wright, David. *Deafness: An Autobiography.* New York: Stein and Day, 1969.

Zazove, Philip. *Four Days in Michigan.* Dallas: Durban House Press, 2009.

Acknowledgments

I wrote this memoir, *The Art of Being Deaf*, with the love and support of many people. I particularly thank my mother, Eloise Helen McDonald.

I am grateful for the financial support provided through the Australian Government's Postgraduate Award, and for the practical support provided by the University of Queensland's School of English, Media Studies and Art History, and in particular, Angela Tuohy.

I thank Julieanne Schultz for publishing my first essay about my deaf girlhood, "I Hear with My Eyes," in *Griffith Review*. With that publication, I discovered the level of interest that readers have about the lives of deaf people.

I thank Stuart Glover and Merv Hyde, who mentored me throughout the entire research and writing process, and Gillian Whitlock for her encouragement.

I thank MaryAnne Baartz for being the ideal first reader: she read each chapter as I wrote it and encouraged me with her laughter and love to hasten to the next chapter. I thank Michelle Dicinoski for her friendship, insights, and cups of coffee with me at Bar Merlo while we were studying and working on our books together.

I thank *all* my friends—some of whom are named in this memoir—for their love and curiosity, necessary ingredients for spurring me ever onward in writing this memoir. I also thank the parents of deaf sons and daughters who read and listened to my stories while I wrote my memoir, in particular Ann Porter, Tina Worland, Helen Wilson, Tina Carter, and Isabel Boura.

Finally, I thank my childhood deaf friends who were such an important part of my early life and who so willingly opened up their hearts in friendship when we met up again in our adult years, and in particular, Sharon Mackay (née Kinnane), Jennifer Holdsworth, Sandra Hoopmann (née Williams), Kay Edgeworth (née Geddes), Kenneth Edgeworth, Matthew Corbett, and Donna Kaye (née Rayward).